NOTES

ON THE

DISTRICT OF GAYA

NOTES

ON THE

DISTRICT OF GAYA

GEORGE A. GRIERSON

GYAN

Published by

Gyan Publishing House
5, Ansari Road
Daryaganj, New Delhi-110002
Phone: 011-47034999, 9811692060
E-mail: books@gyanbooks.com

Distribution Network
gyanbooks.com
India, USA, Canada, UK, Australia

ISBN: 978-93-6780-296-0 (PB)

First Published, 1893

2nd Impression 2024

Printed at: Gyan Press, Delhi.

NOTES ON THE DISTRICT OF GAYA
Author: GEORGE A. GRIERSON

NOTES

ON THE

DISTRICT OF GAYA.

By GEORGE A. GRIERSON, I.C.S.

CALCUTTA:

PRINTED AT THE BENGAL SECRETARIAT PRESS.

1893.

PREFACE.

These notes on the district of Gaya have been compiled by me at different times, as occasion required them, during the past five years.

The volume of the Statistical Account of Bengal relating to that district is far from complete, and what is found here is intended to supplement its deficiencies. It does not, therefore, pretend to be a complete account of the district. Only those subjects are dealt with which a five years' knowledge of the district has shown to me to be ones on which a district officer is likely to want information and concerning which information is not readily accessible.

Although printed at the Government Press, it must be distinctly understood that Government is in no way responsible for any of the opinions or facts brought forward.

In transliterating native words, I have followed the rules laid down in Government Resolution No. 526 Mis., dated 9th February 1892.

G. A. G.
15-1-92.

CONTENTS.

NOTES

ON THE

DISTRICT OF GAYA.

CHAPTER I.

Early History.

THE districts of Gaya and Patna may be taken as roughly corresponding in area with the ancient kingdom of Magadha, which was one of the latest portions of Northern India to come under the civilizing influences of the Aryans. From the oldest Sanskrit writings we learn that Tirhut and Audh contained settled Aryan colonies centuries before Magadha was known at all, except as a geographical expression, and even as late as the compilation of the Atharva Veda it is referred to as a non-Aryan country inhabited by wild tribes hardly worthy of the name of men. To the present day Magadha is known to natives as a country of uncouth inhabitants, "the Bœotia of India."

Even so late as the sixth century before Christ we find Baudháyana mentioning Magadha as a country the inhabitants of which were of mixed origin and outside the pale of Aryan civilization, while the full Aryahood of the people of Tirhut across the Ganges is readily admitted.

During this period, however, the kingdom of Magadha rapidly rose in power. The capital was the Rájagṛiha, the present Rájgir, the first prominent king who reigned there being Bimbisára. He was the Buddha's famous patron, and it was during his reign that the Buddha became enlightened at Bodh Gayá (say 522 B.C.), and founded the Buddhist religion. At that time the city of Patna, which was subsequently to become the capital of Magadha under one of Bimbisára's descendants, was a village lying between the Sone and the Ganges, and was fortified during Buddha's lifetime, under the orders of Bimbisára's son and successor, Ajátaśatru, as a frontier post to repel the incursions of the Vajjians, a Turanian tribe who had entered North Bihár tr ough the Himalayas and had occupied Tirhut.

In those days the Sone entered the Ganges some twenty miles east of its present junction and to the east of Patna, near the present town of Fatua (Fatuhá). Before the junction of the two rivers, which were nearly parallel for many miles, and between them, there was a long narrow tongue of land, on which was fortified Páṭaligráma, the petty village that subsequently grew into Páṭaliputra, Palibothra, or Patna, the famous capital of Bihár. There is reason to believe that the Sone did not burst across this tongue and join the Ganges at its present *embouchure* till about the year 750 A.D.

Under the successors of Bimbisára the power of the Magadha kings gradually extended itself over the whole of Northern India, till they were succeeded about the year 370 B.C. by a low-caste dynasty of Nandas, who added still more to the conquests of their predecessors. They were rooted out by Chandragupta, an illegitimate son of one of the Nandas, who had joined the camp of Alexander the Great on the occasion of his invasion of India. After Alexander's departure, with the help of a well-known Brahman called Cháṇakya, he expelled the Nandas and seized the throne for himself about the year 320 B.C.

Chandragupta, the Sandracottus of the Greeks, kept up intercourse with Alexander's successors, and received at his palace at Páṭaliputra an ambassador of Seleucus Nicator, named Megasthenes, from whom we have received valuable information regarding the extent and powers of the kingdom of Magadha as they existed between the years 317 and 312 B.C. We learn from him that Chandragupta had a large standing army of 600,000 foot soldiers, 30,000 cavalry, and 9,000 elephants, and that he had made himself master of pretty nearly the whole of Northern India. The river Yamuná (Jumna) is specially mentioned as flowing through his kingdom.

Second in succession from Chandragupta was the famous Aśoka (cir. 263 to 222 B.C.), under whom Buddhism was finally adopted as a state religion. His rock and pillar inscriptions in favour of Buddhism contain the earliest pieces of written historical information given in India by an Indian. From them we learn that the whole of Northern India, and even Orissa, were directly subject to his rule, while a great portion of the present Afghanistan, and the Deccan as far south as the river Krishna, were under kings who admitted his over-lordship.

He had relations more or less close with the western world, and he specially mentions as kings with whom he had treaties, and who had admitted Buddhist missionaries to their kingdoms, Antiochus II. of Syria, Ptolemy (Philadelphus) of Egypt, Antigonus Gonatas of Macedonia, Magas of Cyrene, and Alexander of Epirus. It is an interesting fact that he tells us that he had sent to Antiochus, and the kings his neighbours, a selection of medical plants both for men and animals, for at that very time Ptolemy Philadelphus was founding in Egypt the celebrated Alexandrian School of Medicine, from which the learning of our modern nineteenth century doctors takes its starting point. When, therefore, the British Government founds its hospitals in Patna and South Bihár, it is not improbably returning after many days the bread cast upon the waters by the ancient Indian king, who insisted on mercy and tenderness to both man and beast.

After Aśoka the empire of Magadha rapidly declined, and Bṛihadratha, the sixth king from him, was put to death about 183 B.C. by his General, Pushpamitra, who usurped the throne and founded the dynasty of the Śungas, which lasted till about 70 B.C. Devabhúti, the last of the Śungas, was murdered by his Minister, Vasudeva, who founded the Kaṇwa dynasty, which lasted about fifty years.

Magadha was now invaded by the Andhrabhṛityas, a dynasty of Southern India, and was finally conquered by them about the year 25 B.C. From that time it ceased to be an independent kingdom. The rule of the Andhrabhṛityas (of which we have little information) lasted till the middle of the 5th century A.D. Thereafter to the Musalmán conquest, the history of Magadha is almost a blank It was the scene of continual invasions, and that is about all we know.

From the Musalmán conquest the history of Magadha is merged in that of Northern India generally, and needs no special remarks. The Mughal capital of the country was the town of Bihár, the name of which, a relic of ancient times, is a corruption of the Buddhist word *vihára* or monastery. From this town the whole *subah* or province of Bihár took its name.

During British supremacy, up to the year 1865, the greater part of the present Patna district and the north of the present Gaya district formed one district known as zillah Bihár; the south of Gaya, together with a portion of the present Hazáribágh district, being known as zillah Rámgaṛh.

To the present day the Gaya district is composed of two tracts, a northern and a southern, with very distinct characteristics. The northern half of the district, together with the Patna district, is known as Magah, a corruption of Magadha, and is well irrigated and fertile. The southern half, which still locally bears the name of Rámgaṛh, commences about ten miles south of Gaya town, and is still imperfectly irrigated and covered with forests.

Magah represents the ancient Magadha which received Aryan civilization from the north and west and was the area from which Buddhism spread over India. Rámgaṛh has received such civilization as it has got in later years, from the south and south-west.

Magah to the present day is a Buddhist country. It is covered with ruins of temples, and, in frequent fields, Buddhist images are turned up by the plough. It is still affected by strange Buddhist customs, and though Buddhism has disappeared from India, its inhabitants still worship a so-called incarnation of Vishnu whom they call *Baudh Deo.*

Buddhism never seems to have penetrated Rámgaṛh. Indeed during the time of Magadha sovereignty that country must have been a dense forest inhabited only by wild tribes and by a few solitary hermits,—outposts of Aryan civilization. The country is dotted here and there with rude forts which local tradition attributes, and no doubt rightly attributes, to the Kols or wild aboriginal tribes of Central India. In later years clearances were effected in it by enterprising immigrants from Rajputana, who were the ancestors of such Rajput families as those of Deo and Chandragaṛh. By them the south of the district has been brought into cultivation, but this "zillah Rámgaṛh" saw no Buddhist civilization and has no Buddhist remains. Magah is Buddhist, ancient, highly cultivated and thickly populated; Rámgaṛh is Hindu, modern, half-cultivated and sparsely populated.

The zillah of Bihár was surveyed in 1812 by Dr. Buchanan Hamilton. It was at that time divided into twelve police circles, and Dr. Buchanan Hamilton calculated the population of each circle, so far as can be judged, with surprising accuracy, considering that no regular census was taken. He estimated the area at 4,935 square miles, and the population at 2,755,150 persons, of whom 2,030,991 were Hindus and 724,159 Musalmáns. About the year 1837 the police circle of Jahanabad (present population 278,895) was selected by Mr. Adams for his statistical enquiries. He found that it contained 803 villages and 14,953 families, comprising 81,480 souls.

The survey of zillah Bihár (1841—44) gave an area of 5,689 square miles, in which were found 203,312 houses. Since that time, however, two *parganas* (Japtá and Balaunjá), comprising 653 square miles, have been transferred to the Palámau district; the parganas of Bihár and Rájgir, containing 792 square miles, to the Patna district, and pargana Amrito to Monghyr.

In the statistics for 1869, issued by the Board of Revenue, the area of the district is said to be 5,496 square miles, and the population is estimated at 1,470,096, the number of villages at 8,526, and the number of houses at 259,411, of which 12,655 were made of masonry. Of the total population 627,024 were males and 54,091 females; 201,974 were male children under twelve years of age, and 100,957 were female children.

The following table shows the population of the district as ascertained by the censuses of 1872, 1881, and 1891, respectively :—

	Males.	Females.	Total.
1872 ...	953,205	994,619	1,947,824
1881 ...	1,043,441	1,081,241	2,124,682
1891 ...	1,045,011	1,093,320	2,138,331

The Mutiny in Gaya.—The following paragraphs are condensed from Sir J. W. Kaye's *History of the Sepoy War in India*, vol. iii, pp. 151—159:—

"Mr. Tayler, the Commissioner of Patna, on receiving news of the disaster which had befallen Dunbar's relieving party near Arrah, gave orders to the chief officers in his Division to withdraw their establishments into the city of Patna.

"In the month of July 1857 the two chief British officers stationed at Gaya were Mr. Trotter, the Judge, and Mr. Alonzo Money, the Magistrate of Bihár. There had, ever since the commencement of the convulsions in Upper India, been indications in the district of an unquiet spirit pervading more or less all classes of the community, and strongest, perhaps, among the Hindu *zamindars*. In the city itself, the Brahmans had been busy industriously disseminating the fiction, so rife in all parts of the country, of the mixture of the bones or blood of swine and oxen with the *atta*, or flour, in the *bazars*. It seemed to be one of their principal objects to corrupt the Sikh soldiery who were posted there, and to win them over to the rebel cause by these fabrications. When it was found that this was of no avail, they ostracised the Sikhs, declaring them to be Christians. It became necessary to suppress these machinations with a strong hand; so a carpenter, against whom there was proof of having attempted to corrupt two Sikh soldiers, was hanged in the most public manner before all the troops and the police in the place. The example had a salutary effect in the city.

"When news reached Mr. Money that the Dinapore regiments had revolted, he bethought himself of active measures of defence. 'The mutiny of Dinapore,' he wrote to the Bengal Government, 'has thrown Gaya into a ferment. There is nothing, however, to be apprehended from the townspeople. They are surrounded by a new and strong police, and have a wholesome dread of the forty-five English and one hundred Sikhs. The present causes of apprehension are two—the inroad of any large number of Dinapore mutineers, or the approach of the Monghyr and Deoghar Fifth Irregulars, who are sure to rise, I imagine. . . . . If the mutineers, or any portion of them, come this way, they will either remain in the district and be joined by disaffected *zamindars*, or they will make for Gaya. There are plenty of *zamindars* who would join them, if they once got the upper hand; but none, I think, that will hazard life and property before that. The following is our plan of operations:—Any body of the mutineers under 300 or 350 are to be met about two miles from the town; 45 English, 100 Sikhs, and 40 *najíbs*, besides four or five residents, will oppose them. I shall put the *najíbs* between the Sikhs and the English, so they must be staunch or be cut to pieces. The mutineers would be dejected and tired after a long march, and I have no doubt of giving them a good thrashing. If they come in large numbers, I shall place the treasure in a brick-house, which is being provisioned, and we will defend it with the same numbers as above.'

"Affairs were in this state when news of Dunbar's disaster having reached Patna, Mr. Tayler issued the orders of which I have above spoken. How those orders were received at Gaya cannot be better told than in the words of the Magistrate himself:—

"'On the 31st of July,' wrote Mr. Alonzo Money not long afterwards, 'I was sitting in my room, talking to the *subahdár* of the *najíbs*, when a letter, marked 'urgent' and 'express,' was put into my hands. I opened it: it was from the Commissioner. It contained a telegraph message from the Government, and an order for me. The message spoke of the defeat of Dunbar's party near Arrah, and continued: 'Everything must now be sacrificed to holding the country and the occupation of a central position.' The order desired me and the other civil authorities to come with all our force to Patna, making our arrangements as promptly and quickly as possible. It contained an injunction to remove the treasure, if doing so endangered not personal safety. 'What does the Commissioner Sahib say?' asked the *subahdár*. I made some excuse, and after a minute or two sent him off. I then despatched a circular round the station, and within an hour every one was present. It was agreed that we should start at five that evening. . . . . At six we started.' They went, leaving everything behind them—seven or eight *lákhs* of rupees in the treasury, and a gaol gorged with criminals; leaving the station and all that it contained under the charge of the *daroga* and the *subahdár* of the *najíbs*, and set their faces towards Patna in obedience to the orders they had received. But the orders were that they should not abandon the treasure unless their lives were endangered by the attempt to remove it; and there were those at Gaya who thought that they might have safely remained to complete their measures for the safe custody of the coin.

"But they had not ridden more than two or three miles when Alonzo Money fell into conversation with a gentleman of the Uncovenanted Service named Hollings. He was an officer attached to the Opium Agency, and he had no duty demanding his return to Gaya; but he felt acutely the degradation of the sudden abandonment of the station. Mr. Money was moved by kindred feelings. So these two brave men determined to return to Gaya and see what could be done to save the property of the Government and lessen the discredit of this precipitate retreat. Whilst, therefore, the rest went on to Patna, Money and Hollings went back to the station which they had so lately quitted. They found things nearly as they had left them. The treasure remained intact, the gaol held fast its prisoners. Up to this time the *najíbs* had faithfully fulfilled their trust. The return of the Magistrate seemed to give confidence to the people. Many of the most respectable inhabitants waited on Mr. Money and welcomed him back with expressions of joy. But when, as a measure of precaution, not unwise in itself, he burnt the Government stamped paper, the first feeling of confidence subsided, and presently the *najibs* rose against us.

"It was now plain that the position of these gallant Englishmen was one of no common difficulty and danger. Not only was there, as far as their information then extended, a prospect of being visited by the Dinapore mutineers and the insurgent rabble under Kuar Singh, but they were threatened more imminently by an incursion of mutineers from Hazáribágh, where the native troops had also revolted. The first step, therefore, to be taken was to recall the detachment of Her Majesty's Sixty-fourth, which had left Gaya just before the European exodus; and this done, the treasure was to be secured. Every effort was made to collect carriage for the transport of the coin, and on the 4th of August the convoy was ready to depart. But in what direction was it to proceed? The order (it has been shown) which Money had received was that he should convey the treasure to Patna, if it could be done without endangering European life. And this was the course which in the first instance he had resolved to pursue. But when false rumours came from Dinapore that a body of mutineers was marching on Gaya and that martial law had been proclaimed in all the Bihár districts, there seemed to be little hope of so small a party, heavily encumbered, reaching Patna in safety. It was determined, therefore, at a council of civil and military officers, that the better course would be to take the Grand Trunk Road to Calcutta—a far longer, but a safer journey. So the treasure party moved out from Gaya, under command of Captain Thompson.

"That night the little party was attacked by a mixed crowd of gaol-birds and gaolers. The escaped prisoners, and the *najibs* who should have forbidden their escape, had made the expected combination, and had come to seize the treasure. Although it was a night attack, it was not a surprise. Thompson's men were ready for them, and they gave the would-be plunderers a warm reception: some of them were shot down, and the rest were glad to carry their lives back with them to Gaya. From that time Money went on his way uninterrupted and unmolested; and in the middle of August he rode into Calcutta, and delivered over to Government the large amount of treasure which he had rescued from the clutches of the insurgents. Amongst the exploits of the war scored down to the credit of the Bengal Civil Service, there are few which at the time excited more enthusiasm than this. The Governor-General and his colleagues commended the conduct of Alonzo Money, and sent him back to Gaya with enlarged responsibilities and increased emoluments. Mr. Hollings also had substantial reasons for knowing that his conduct was approved by the higher authorities."

In the mutiny, amongst other buildings, the public record-room was burnt down, and all its valuable contents looted or destroyed. The only official records of the district which go back beyond 1857 are those of the subdivision of Nawádah, which the native officials hid in a cave in a neighbouring hill when the insurgents destroyed the local offices. These records are still in existence, but have never been properly arranged since they were brought back from their temporary hiding place in a disorganised state. Hence any detailed account of their contents is impossible. Enough has been seen by the present writer to satisfy him that they will give valuable information to any future local historian who has plenty of leisure time.

CHAPTER II.

The Geography of the District.

THE general aspect of the district is a level plain, with a ridge of hills winding in a serpentine form along the southern boundary, whence the country falls with a gentle slope towards the Ganges in the north. The surface is interrupted here and there by rocky hills, either isolated or in groups, which seldom exceed 1,000 feet in height. They are composed of granular silicious hornstone granites, mixed with white quartz and loose masses of iron ore. The larger ones are covered with jungle and coarse grass; the rest are rocky and bare.

The eastern portion of the district, comprising chiefly the subdivision of Nawádah, and the northern and western portions, comprising pargana Sanaut in the Sadar subdivision and parganas Ikkil, Arwal, Okrí, and Bheláwar in the Jahanabad subdivision, are highly cultivated and extensively irrigated by artificial means maintained at heavy cost. The north-eastern portion of the latter subdivision is becoming less fertile owing to the silting up of the Muháná river opposite the Barábar hills, near Ibrábímpur, while the remainder of the district, including the southern part of Aurangabad subdivision, consists of hills and jungles abounding with wild animals. This part of the country used to be thinly peopled and not much cultivated; but of late years much of the jungle has been cleared away, and the cultivated area is rapidly increasing. The soil is generally alluvial. Towards the north and west it consists of *kewál*, a species of clay; *paurú*, composed of sand and clay; and *rehrá*, or white soil, which is good for paddy only. About Sherghati it is sandy. To the west, between the Sone and Punpun rivers, the soil is generally of a light nature, and very productive. The rivers all run from south to north. With the exception of the Sone and Punpun, they are little better than hill torrents, being as a rule dry beds throughout the greater portion of the year. There are fine groves of trees in all parts of the district, especially between the Sone and the Punpun.

Rivers.—The Sone.—The principal river in the district is the Sone (more properly spelt Són), which forms the boundary between the districts of Gaya and Shahabad. It contains water at all seasons, and in every part of its course; and its channel is, in general, almost equal in size to that of the Ganges. After heavy rains this channel is nearly filled, and the rapidity of the current is such as to be scarcely compatible with navigation up-stream; but generally during the rainy season boats of twenty tons burthen can traverse the whole extent of this district. At the village of Bárun, where the Grand Trunk Road cuts the Sone, the river is crossed by a causeway, which is under water during the rains. Just above this is the head of the Sone Canal works. The general aspect of the river during the heats of the spring is desert; and its eastern bank is in many parts overwhelmed with sandy barren downs, blown up from its channel. The bed is nowhere rocky, but with the golden-coloured (or rather ruddy-coloured) sand (from which the name of the river is derived) are intermixed a variety of small pebbles, some of which are very ornamental. This stream is too deeply sunk in its channel to be of any use in irrigating the adjacent country; but this defect has been remedied by the canal works. Dr. Buchanan-Hamilton thinks that "Patna may possibly have been once at the junction of the Sone with the Ganges, but there is no tradition among the natives concerning such a circumstance." This point has since been decided conclusively in the affirmative by Mr. Ravenshaw and General Cunningham. Traces of old courses of the Sone were also noticed by the officers engaged on the Patna Canal; and one of these courses has been used in laying out the line of the canal. Mr. Bourdillon, C.S., gives as an additional proof that the village Nadí, on the edge of one of these old channels, now some ten miles from the nearest point of the Sone, is mentioned in some exceedingly old and curious documents of the Delhi empire as *Nadí ba-lab-i-daryá Son*—Nadí on the Sone brink. Under the name of Erannoboas this river is mentioned by Megasthenes, whose account has been preserved by Arrian, "as the third river throughout all India, and inferior to none but the Indus and the Ganges, into the latter of which it discharges its water." Erannoboas was the Greek form of Hiraṇyabáhá, a name taken from the river's golden (or rather ruddy) waters. The Sone rises in the highlands of Amarkaṇṭak, and flows through a country possessing a reddish, gravelly soil. In the floods the river necessarily brings down large volumes of the red dust and sand, which it deposits in the deeper pools. In the cold season this deposit, seen through the clear waters, gives them a distinct tinge of red.

The question of the ancient course of the Sone was finally decided in 1872-73, and the results, together with the reasoning on which they are based, will be found discussed at great length in Volume VIII of the Reports of the Archæological Survey of India. It is conclusively shown that in ancient times the Sone only followed its present course as far as TARÁṚH near DAUDNAGAR, and thence travelled north-east, *viâ* RÁMPUR-CHÁÍ, KAYÁL, and DEOKUṆḌ to SIDHRÁMPUR and SON BHADR on the river PUNPUN. From thence it followed the present course of the Punpun, being joined on the way by the MORHAR about four miles west of the present town of JAHANABAD, to CHILBIL, south of PHULWÁRÍ and close to the present Dinapore railway station, in the Patna district. Thence it turned east as far as PÁNCH-PAHÁRÍ in Patna city, and then to the south-east, finally joining the Ganges at Fatuhá (the Fatua station of the East Indian Railway). There is a long tract of low ground in this last direction, destitute of trees, and the inundation waters of the Sone, Punpun, and Morhar still find their way down this old bed to the Ganges. This is the old channel to which Buchanan gives the name of MAR-SON, the dead, or deserted Sone. The courses of the Ganges and Sone would thus have been nearly parallel for many miles, and in this narrow tract lying between the two rivers was situated the famous city of Páṭaliputra or Palibothra, the ancient Patna, and the then capital of the Gangetic provinces. As years went on, the Sone gradually worked westwards, its lower course at length closely approximating its present condition as far as Phulwárí, and it is probable that the final catastrophe, in which the Sone, instead of turning east at that point, burst across the narrow neck of land, there situated, into the Ganges, took place shortly before the year 750 A.D. This last point is, however, doubtful, and depends on the correct interpretation of certain Chinese records. In the annexed map, the black dotted line shows approximately the old course of the Sone.

Ferries across the Sone are situated opposite the following places:—Arwal, Daudnagar, Bárun, and Akbarpur in the district of Shahabad.

The Punpun.—Eastwards from the Sone the next river is the Punpun, which rises in the extreme south of the district and flows towards the Ganges in a north-easterly course, more or less parallel to that of the Sone. As above explained, a great portion of its course is really the old bed of that river. During the driest part of the year there is always some stream; and the water is most extensively used by the adjacent villages for irrigation purposes. Small channels, called *pains*, often continuing for a considerable distance, distribute the river water over the fields, or flow into large public reservoirs, *áhars*, where the water is stored until required by the cultivators. The Punpun receives many small feeders on its right bank, of which the Dháwá, Batáná, and Madár are the chief. These streams dry up during the hot weather; and even when full, the greater part of their water never reaches the Punpun, having been dispersed over the fields by artificial channels.

Map showing

THE ANCIENT COURSE OF THE SONE AND THE ANCIENT LINES OF COMMUNICATION IN MAGADHA.

Scale 1 Inch = 32 Miles.

20 15 10 5 0 20 Miles

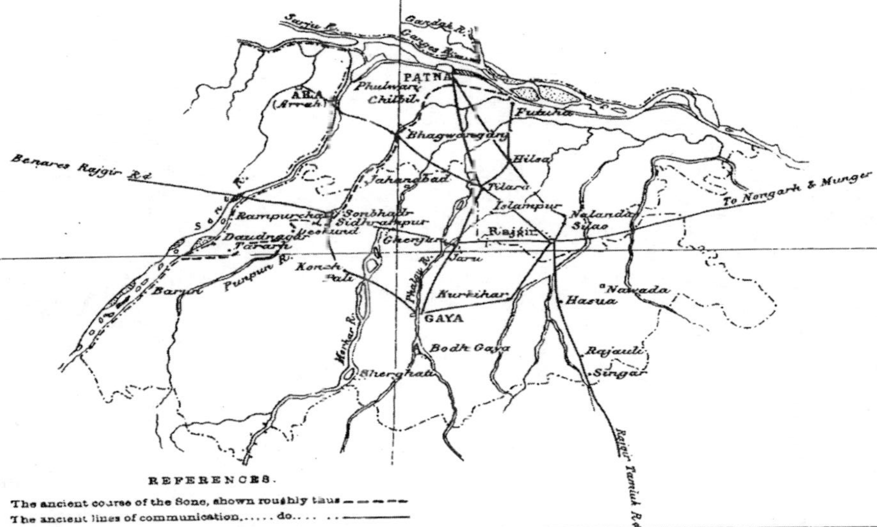

REFERENCES.

The ancient course of the Sone, shown roughly thus — — — —

The ancient lines of communication, ... do. . . . . . ————

Reg. No 3?, Pandal, Finl.—Feb 02 – ?

Litho., S. I. O., Calcutta.

Other tributaries of the Punpun do not join it in this district; for example, the Morhar, which, coming from the south, flows northwards past the important towns of Sherghati (at one time the head-quarters of a subdivision) and Tikari, the capital of the Tikari Ráj. At Tikari this river divides into two branches, of which the easternmost, called the Dardhá, flows past Jahanabad, and during the rainy season floods a large tract of country round that place. Some high land to the north forces the excess of water to disperse itself over this part of the district. Another stream, the Jamuná, flows from the south, between Gaya and Tikari; it then flows east and passes the Patna road at Makhdúmpur, and on beyond Ṭeh̤ṭá, where it twists back and joins the Dardhá at Jahanabad.

The *Phálgú*, flowing north and south, intersects the district. It is formed a few miles above Gaya town by the union of two hill-torrents, the Liláján and Muháná, which both enter the district from the south. When the Phálgú reaches the high and rocky shores of Gaya it is above 900 yards wide, and for the next half mile is remarkable for its sanctity. During the hot weather it dries up, but water can always be obtained by digging a few feet below the surface. After leaving Gaya the river runs in a north-easterly direction for about 17 miles. When opposite the Barábar hills it divides into two branches, which flow eventually into a branch of the Punpun. It is there again called the Muháná.

The east of the district is drained by a number of small streams, which all unite near Giriyak, at the eastern corner of Patna district. The more important of these are called the Ḍháḍhar, Tilaiyá, Dhanárjay, Khurí, and Sakrí. They are very useful for irrigation, but do not require any further description.

Changes in the river courses.—The changes in the course of the Sone have been already mentioned. In the other streams, also, the changes have been frequent. The volume of water varies continually, and the system of irrigation practised by the cultivators all over the district is perpetually modifying the river courses. Dr. Buchanan-Hamilton mentions more than one instance where he was unable to find streams of the description given by Major Rennel, and the last sixty years have rendered Major Rennel's survey still more incorrect.

The banks of the rivers are in general low and sloping; the beds are of pure sand. Towards the hills the banks become more abrupt, and the beds are often rocky. The sudden rise and fall of these petty rivers is remarkable. A heavy downpour of rain will render a shallow stream unfordable in a few hours; and, as a rule, no boats are obtainable. The country people, however, provide a ready substitute in the shape of a light raft (*gharnái*), made of light bamboos floated on inverted earthenware pots (*ghará*). Such a raft, though flimsy in appearance, is strong enough to bear the weight of a *pálkí*, and a man swims across the river with the tow-rope in his mouth.

Lakes and marshes.—Throughout the district there is nothing that can be called a lake, and the marshes, properly speaking, are of trifling extent During the rains, however, much of the country is artificially converted into marsh land for rice cultivation.

River traffic.—There are no towns or villages in this district the population of which live exclusively by river traffic. What traffic there is, is confined to the Sone, on which the two chief towns are Daudnagar and Arwal. From both of these places country produce is sent down the river. Dr. Buchanan-Hamilton mentions that some timber and bamboos were floated down in rafts, but that far the greater part of the exports and imports, even in the vicinity of the Sone, were effected by land carriage. There is a steamer service on the Eastern Sone Canal, which does the entire trip from Bárun to Khagaul, near Dinapore, and *vice versâ,* in about two days. It carries a large quantity of goods.

Canals.—Twenty years ago there were no canals in this district, but now (1890) it is traversed by two important lines, viz., the Eastern Main Canal and the Patna Canal. About half a mile south of the causeway which carries the Grand Trunk Road across the Sone from Bárun to Dehri (Ḍihurí) two main canals branch off, one from each side of the river.

All the information that could be collected about the Sone Canal works has been embodied in one account, which will be found in the statistical account of Shahabad district. Only a few points exclusively affecting the district of Gaya will be mentioned here. The Eastern Main Canal was originally designed to convey water for the irrigation of the whole area as far as Monghyr, but the work has not been continued beyond the Punpun, a distance of 8 miles. To divert the water into this canal an *anicut,* or weir, has been built across the river. Four miles from the Sone the Patna Canal branches off from the Eastern Main Canal, and following, as far as possible, the direction of the Sone, joins the Ganges near the old jail at Díghá, a village between Bankipore and Dinapore. This canal is 79 miles long, and commands an area of 780 square miles, or 499,200 acres. Of the whole length 43 miles lie in this district, and the remaining 36 miles are in Patna. They are in full working order. It may be added that during the famine of 1873-74 these works not only gave employment to numbers of labourers, amounting at one time to over 40,000 persons, but the water which was passed through the unfinished channels irrigated nearly 160,000 acres, increasing the food-supply by 70,000 tons.

Fisheries.—The fisheries in this district are unimportant, and are not preserved, except to some extent by the Gaya Municipality. The census of 1872 returns the number of men employed in fishing at 1,070, or about ·05 per cent. of the population. The figures for the census of 1891 were not available when this was written. The truth is that there are none who live only by fishing, while all the low castes catch fish at certain seasons for their own consumption. There are plenty of fish in the Sone, but very few are caught, for in the rainy season the stream is too violent, and in the dry season the water is in general so shallow and clear that the simple and imperfect means used by the native fishermen are quite useless. It has been estimated that about fifty-three tons of fish are caught every year throughout the district, of which perhaps one-third are obtained at Gaya town. In the other rivers of the district numbers of small fish are caught when the water subsides. So also in the tanks, and even in the rice-fields which have been artificially flooded. It is not easy to account for the swarms of little fish which are found on these fields in August. Some, of course, find their way from the rivers during the rains, through the rills and artificial watercourses; but these means seem inadequate to account for the numbers of fish that appear. Dr. Buchanan-Hamilton thought that the greater part are bred from eggs that remain dry in the soil until hatched by the heat and moisture of the rainy season.

Line of drainage.—The drainage of the district runs invariably from south to north, from the Hazáribágh plateau to the Ganges valley. Its sweep is marked, not by *jhíls* or marshes, but by the broad sandy beds of the hill torrents. In the south, the drainage at first falls abruptly from the boundary range; afterwards the slope is more gradual, being about six feet per mile up to twenty miles north of Gaya town, and thence only two feet per mile to the Ganges. About Jahanabad the land is slightly depressed; and during the floods the Jamuná inundates a large tract of country at its junction with the Dardhá. The extreme south-west of the district is drained by the Sone through the Koil.

Hills.—It has been already mentioned that isolated hills may be seen in most parts of the district. The highest of these, called Maher (*Mahá-giri*), is situated about 12 miles to the south-east of Gaya town, and rises from a spreading plain to a height of 1,620 feet above the sea. South of the Jahanabad subdivision are the Barábar hills, a remarkable cluster of rounded elevations. In the *Bengal Atlas* of Major Rennel this cluster is called the Currumshaw hills. Dr. Buchanan-Hamilton points out that this name is a corruption of *Karan chaupár*, or Karna's seat, the name of one of the ancient caves on these hills. About two miles to the west of the Barábar hills is the remarkable isolated hill of Kauwá Ḍol. These are more fully described in dealing with the Jahanabad subdivision.

There is another remarkable cluster or ridge of hills on the east side of the river Phálgú, which runs about west-south-west and east-north-east for a considerable way, forming part of the boundary between the districts of Patna and Gaya. The chief archæological interest attached to these hills centres round Rájagṛiha, which belongs more properly to the Patna side, and is described in the statistical account of that district. But the southern part of this ridge, which lies within the district of Gaya, has many remarkable peaks, which are alluded to by Hiuen Tsiang, the Chinese pilgrim who visited India in the seventh century of the Christian era. These spots have been identified by General Cunningham, who gives a most interesting account of them in his *Ancient Geography*. The pilgrim, on his way from Bodh Gayá to Rájagṛiha, mentions the hill of Kiu-kiu-cha-po-tho, the Chinese corruption of Kukkaṭa-páda-giri, or Hill of the Cock's Foot. It is identified by General Cunningham with the village of Kuṛkíhár, which is three miles to the north-east of Wazírganj. The true name of Kuṛkíhár is said to be Kuṛakbihár, which is the Hindi form of the Sanskrit name Kukkaṭa-vihára, or Cock's temple. About 17 miles to the north-east of this is another hill, called by the pilgrim Fo-to-fa-na, *i.e.*, Buddhavana, which is probably the modern Budhain.

The only other remarkable ridge is the one which forms the southern boundary of the district. The summits are of no great height, but are prettily wooded, and were formerly full of game. It is in these hills that the rivers and streams which intersect the district take their rise. They may be considered as a part of the Vindhyan mountains, by which the great Gangetic plain is bounded on the south.

Mineral Products.—The following paragraphs are chiefly condensed from the elaborate account given by Dr. Buchanan-Hamilton :—The southern range of hills is composed of igneous rocks. The prevailing minerals vary in their proportion, but generally speaking these hills contain quartz, red, white and granular jasper, hornblende, and mica. Mines of the latter mineral have been worked for some years at Sapahí, about 15 miles south-east of Rajaulí, by Babu Drigopál Lál of Hasuá, and also at Síngar, about 6 miles south-west of the same place, by Messrs. Christien & Co., of Calcutta. They are said not to yield a profit now, but the fact of their existence at all leads to the conclusion that they must have done so at the commencement of mining operations. The mica is sent to Calcutta, whence it is exported to Europe and America for various purposes. As the mineral is known also to exist in the Government estates of Chaṭkarí and Dubaur in the neighbourhood of Rajaulí, licenses have lately been issued to enable persons interested in the trade to prospect for it. No trustworthy statistics of the outturn of the mines at Sapahí and Síngar are available. Iron also is found in Pachambá in the east of Nawádah subdivision in lumps on the surface of the earth or at a very slight depth below the surface. About 100 *mans* (3⅓ tons), valued at £20, are worked yearly. The metal is found mixed with earth, from which it is freed by boiling. It is then worked up by the people and manufactured into rude implements of agriculture.

The long cluster of hills commencing near Bodh Gayá, which forms eventually the boundary between the districts of Gaya and Patna, is also igneous. The south of the range consists of jasper, red and white, while further north there is an admixture of quartz. There are no mines in any of these hills. The third great cluster of minerals among the Barábar hills consists chiefly of granite, without any vestige of stratification. This stone is quarried by the poorest classes for mending the Patna and Gaya road. Iron ore is found in small masses lying loose at the bottom of some of these hills. The southern part of this group towards Gaya is famous for a quarry of black pot-stone. This is polished and carved into vases and figures of animals, which form one of the *spécialités* of the district. The ornamental pebbles which are found in the bed of the Sone have been already mentioned. Calcareous nodules are found near the banks of the rivers, and the saline efflorescence, from which saltpetre is manufactured, is common in many villages.

Ancient Lines of Communication.—Ancient MAGADHA, which roughly corresponds to the modern districts of PATNA and GAYA, was traversed by several important lines of communication connecting North-Western India with Rájgir and with the Bay of Bengal. There was also a large amount of traffic between the cities of GAYA and PATNA. The following information is condensed from that given in Volume VIII of the Reports of the Archæological Survey of India. The lines of communication will be found marked on the map opposite page 10:—

The old Gaya-Patna road ran along the east bank of the river Phálgú from Gaya northwards, passing close to Islámpur and Tiláṛá through Hilsá. From Tiláṛá, however, a road must once have gone direct to Patna, as the Chinese pilgrim Hiuen Tsiang travelled by it from that city. It must have been a difficult one, involving a crossing of the ancient Sone, and most of the traffic probably went along the easier road *viâ* Hilsá and Fatua, which must have been a somewhat important port.

The Banáras-Rájgir road seems to have crossed the old Sone at Sone Bhadr, the Morhar at Ghenjan, and the Phálgú and the Patna-Gaya road at Járú.

The Árá (Arrah)-Rájgir road seems to have crossed the old Sone at Bhagwánganj, the Phálgú at Tiláṛá and passed through or close to Islámpur.

The Patna-Rájgir road probably crossed the old Sone somewhere near Fat'hpur Kalán. It then crossed the Phálgú and the Fatua branch of the Gaya-Patna road at Hilsá, and passed through Nálandá and Siláo.

The Gaya-Banáras road seems to have struck the Banáras-Rájgir road at Sone Bhadr on the old Sone, and passing through Konch, crossed the Morhar at Pálí to avoid two branches of the river, which it would have had to meet if it had crossed either above or below.

The Rájgir-Tamlúk road, connecting the Bay of Bengal with the North-West, probably entered Gaya district *viâ* the Síngar pass and Rajauli.

The Banáras-Tamlúk road probably went through Palámau and Ranchi.

SADAR, OR HEAD-QUARTERS SUBDIVISION.

The population of the subdivision is 832,442, of whom 407,568 are males and 424,874 females. There is only one town, Tikari, in this subdivision, besides Gaya, which has a population exceeding 5,000 persons.

Gaya (more accurately spelt Gayá) city, being fully described in the statistical account of the district, is not dealt with here. The population of the municipality in 1891 was 80,383, of whom 40,893 were males and 39,490 females.

The country immediately round Gaya city comprises the jurisdiction of the GAYA MUFASSAL police-station, the head-quarters of which are situated about a mile from Gaya, on the east side of the river Phálgú. Its police staff consists of 1 sub-inspector, 1 head-constable, and 10 constables. It has three outposts—at WAZÍRGANJ, an important mart 15 miles east of Gaya; at PARAIYÁ, 12 miles west, on the river Morhar; and at BODH GAYÁ, 7 miles south, respectively.

The population of the police jurisdiction is 180,017, of whom 87,929 are males and 92,088 females.

BODH GAYÁ, which is situated a few hundred yards to the west of the river Phálgú or Lílájan, is without doubt one of the most interesting historical sites in the world. It was under the sacred fig-tree here that Sakya Siñha received enlightenment, and became "the Buddha" (or "enlightened one"). The village is hence the birth-place of the Buddhist religion, and the holiest place in existence to one-third of the inhabitants of the earth. The writer avoids any detailed description of the famous temple built over the spot where the Buddha sat when the divine message came to him, for any account which could be contained within the limits of these notes would necessarily be incomplete and give a wrong impression. Dr. Rajendra Lal Mittra and General Cunningham have each devoted a whole volume to its history and architecture, to which those interested must be referred. A brief account will also be found on pages 53 and ff. of the Statistical Account of Gaya. Suffice it to say here that the present temple is undoubtedly the same as that seen and described by the Chinese pilgrim, Hiuen Tsiang, in the seventh century A.D., and was probably built a century before him. The special attention of the visitor may be directed to the famous Aśóka railings, some of which are still in position, which date from the third century B.C., and originally surrounded an older temple, on the site of which the existing one was built. Some of the sculptures on the pillars of this railing show distinct traces of Greek art.

Independently of the great Buddhist temple, the *maṭh*, or Sivite monastery close by, and in whose land it stands, demands more than a passing notice. It is inhabited by a sect of *Dasnámí Sannyásís*, the ten orders of which were founded by Sankara Áchárya. The Bodh Gayá sect is styled *Gir*. The founder is said to have been Gosain Ghamaṇḍí Gir, who came here in the year 1590 A.D., and, attracted by the beauty of the spot, built a small monastery. He was the first *mahanth* or abbot. The present mahanth, Gosain Kṛishṇa Dayál Gir, is twelfth in descent from him. Among his predecessors may be mentioned the third mahanth, Gosain Mahádeva Gir (1642—1682). Tradition says that he worshipped Anna Púrná, the Goddess of Plenty, who, pleased by his devotion, presented him with a wondrous cup for the distribution of grain, the virtue of which was such that so long as alms were distributed by the mahanths from it, the monastery would never lack. Moreover, its contents were always sufficient to exactly satisfy the appetite of the recipient of the alms dealt from it, be he man or woman, child or adult, full or hungry. This cup (*kaṭorá*) is still in existence, and is used daily for the distribution of alms to the numerous pilgrims who pass by the monastery. It was during the time of this mahanth that the present large monastery was built. Subsequent mahanths received valuable presents of land from the Emperor of Delhi and others, for which *farmáns* are still shown.

The tenth mahanth, Gossain Bhaipati Gir, rendered service to the English in the mutiny of 1857. He died in 1867 and was succeeded by Hem Náráyan Gir, a learned man, who managed his important trust with liberality and discretion. In consideration of his services in the famine of 1873-74, he was granted a Certificate of Honour on the occasion of the proclamation of Her Majesty's title of Empress of India. He died at Banáras, universally regretted, on the 27th December 1891, when he was succeeded by the present mahanth, Gosain Kṛishṇa Dayál Gir.

The succession to the see of the mahanthship is, according to custom, determined by election. When a mahanth dies, five of his followers are nominated as *panches*, or electors, by the general body of disciples. These select as the successor, the disciple whom they consider most learned, most pious, and most capable. The person chosen is then formally installed on the *gaddí* or throne of the monastery, and each disciple presents him with a sheet in token of acceptance of his supremacy.

The following is a list of the mahanths of Bodh Gayá, since the foundation of the monastery in 1590 :—

(1) Ghamaṇḍí Gir (1590—1615).
(2) Chaitanya Gir (1615—1642).
(3) Mahádeva Gir (1642—1682).
(4) Lalá Gir (1682— ?).
(5) Keshav Gir (? —1748).
(6) Rághav Gir (1748—1769).
(7) Rám Hit Gir (1769—1806).
(8) Bálak Gir (1806—1820).
(9) Siv Gir (1820—1846).
(10) Bhaipati Gir (1846—1867).
(11) Hem Náráyan Gir (1867—1891).
(12) Kṛishṇa Dayál Gir (1891, now living).

Bakraur, on the Phálgú, opposite Bodh Gayá, was visited by the Chinese pilgrim Hiuen Tsiang, who relates a story regarding the capture by a certain king of a "scented elephant" (*gandha-hasti*). In a former existence, Buddha was said to have been a son of this elephant, and a *stupa* and pillar had accordingly been erected in commemoration of this tradition. There was also a sacred tank. The ruins of the stupa still exist in the shape of a large mound called Kataní, which has been several times dug into for treasure. About the year 1790 numerous lac seals were found in it. The stump of the pillar, which is still *in situ*, is about three feet in diameter. According to General Cunningham, the shaft of the pillar is said to have been taken to Gaya by a former Magistrate, and to be a column now existing at the centre of Sáhibganj or the new town of Gaya, bearing a Persian inscription attributing its setting up to Mr. Charles Boddam, in A.D. 1789. The sacred tank is probably represented by a small walled tank now called *Mártaṇḍ Pokhar*, or *Suraj Kuṇḍ*, *i.e.*, "Tank of the Sun." An annual fair is held by it, which thousands of pilgrims attend, to bathe in its sacred waters. The ancient name of Bakraur is said to have been Ajayapura.

On the Gaya-Nawádah road, fourteen miles to the east of Gaya, between two hills of grey granite, is the village of Punáwáñ, where there are two tanks, and several old Buddhist remains. The principal object was formerly a pillared temple of Triloknáth, but it has been destroyed by people who found the richly sculptured pillars useful as gate-posts. A mile to the south-east of Punáwáñ are two small isolated ranges of hills close to each other. The valley between them is known as the Kol, and the place itself is known as Hasrá. Hasrá has the remains of some very fine old tanks. The valley is thickly studded with mounds and with fragments of Buddhist carvings and architecture. Across the east end, where it is narrowest, are built two lines of massive stone walls. Numerous statues of large size, and in excellent preservation, have been exhumed from the mounds and carried off to the village of Bishunpur Tañrwáñ, within the boundary of which the Kol is situated, about a mile further to the south. One of these is a seated statue of Buddha. The ruins at Punáwáñ and Hasrá are said, by tradition, to have been built by a Rájá called by some Tilóknáth, and by others Banautí Rájá. To the south-east of Bishunpur Ṭañrwáñ, on a rocky eminence called Sobhnathiyá, are some ruins, said to be the *gaṛh* or foot of a Rájput Chief named Sobh Náth.

About three miles north-east of Wazírganj lies the village of Kuṛkíhár, which is specially interesting as the probable site of the old *Kukkuṭa-páda-giri* (or "Cock's-foot-hill") Buddhist monastery, also visited by Hiuen Tsiang on his way from Bodh Gayá to Rájgir *viâ* Tapoban. There are several lofty mounds in and round the village, which have been hitherto but slightly explored, the largest being to its south; but the monastery is now represented by a high mound to the north. This mound is called to the present day *Sugat-ghar* (the house of Sugat), *Sugat* being one of the well-known titles of Buddha. About half a mile to the north of the village three bare and rugged hills rise boldly out of the plain. They are said to have been the scene of some of the miracles of the Buddhist saint *Mahá-kasyapa*, and eventually of his *nirváṇa* or death. The Chinese pilgrim Fa Hian tells us that in his time (A.D. 400) the hills were thickly wooded and were full of lions, tigers, and wolves, so that travellers had to be cautious. This part of the country is still infested by leopards, and now and then, also by tigers. Kuṛkíhár is actually within the boundary of Atari thána, but may be most conveniently visited from Wazírganj.

Other villages within the jurisdiction of this thána, and which may be mentioned, are Deokuli, Chákan (on the Patna-Gayá Railway) and Kenárchaṭṭí. Pret Silá, or "Ghost's rock," is a rude piece of stone marked with a gold line, before which pilgrims place *piṇḍás*, or offerings, for the repose of the manes (or *pretas*) of their ancestors. It is on the top of a hill about 400 feet high, five miles north-west of Gaya. There are also here four temples and three tanks.

Tikari (or more accurately Ṭekárí) is situated on the river Morhar, about 15 miles to the north-west of Gaya, in 24° 56′ 38″ N. latitude and 84° 52′ 53″ E. longitude. According to the census of 1891, Tikari contains a population of 11,532 persons, of whom 5,381 are males and 6,151 are females. The gross municipal income for the year 1887-88 was Rs. 11,435-12-3, and the expenditure for the same period

Rs. 6,178-1-4; the rate of the municipal taxation being 7½ per cent. on annual value of the holdings. The local police consists of 1 head-constable and 23 constables for town duty only, besides 1 sub-inspector, 1 head-constable, and 12 constables for regular police duty. The population of the police jurisdiction is 184,654, of whom 90,752 are males and 93,902 females.

Tikari is the head-quarters of the well-known Tikari family. The founder was one Dhír Singh, a small landed proprietor. His son, Sundar Singh, took advantage of the confusion occasioned by the invasion of Nádir Sháh to build up the Ráj by the forcible acquisition of the mahâls in his vicinity, and was granted the title of Rájá by the Mughal Government. His adopted son, Buniád Singh, succeeded to the property, and was also created a Rájá by the same power.

Buniád Singh was succeeded by his son Mitarjít Singh, who was created Mahárája by the British Government. He had two sons, Hit Náráyan and Mód Náráyan, and by his will divided the property between them, giving the former (the elder) a 9 annas and the latter a 7 annas share. The present representative of the elder or 9 annas branch of the family is Mahárâj Kumár Gopál Saran Náráyan Singh, a minor under the Court of Wards. Rájá Ran Bahádur Singh, the representative of the younger or 7 annas branch, died in 1890, and the succession is now under dispute, his grand-daughter, Rájkumári Ratan Kuar, being at present in possession.

The following is a genealogical tree of the family:—

DHI'R SINGH.

- RÁJÁ SUNDAR SINGH, (*son*).
  - RÁJÁ BUNIÁD SINGH, (*adopted son*).
    - MAHÁRÁJ MITARJÍT SINGH, (*son*). (died in 1840).
      - MAHÁRÁJ HIT NÁRÁYAN SINGH, (*son*).
        - MAHÁRÁNÍ INDARJIT KUAR, (*wife*).
          - MAHÁRÁJ RÁM KISHUN SINGH, (*adopted son*), (died in 1875).
            - MAHÁRÁNÍ RÁJRÚP KUAR, (*daughter*).
              - MAHÁRÁNÍ RADHÉSWARÍ KISHORI KUAR, (*daughter*). (died in 1886).
                - MAHÁRÁJ KUMÁR GOPÁL SARAN NÁRÁYAN SINGH, *minor son, the present proprietor*).
      - RÁJÁ MÓD NÁRÁYAN SINGH, (*son*).
        - RÁNÍ ASMEDH KUAR, (*wife*).
          - RÁJÁ RAN BAHÁDUR SINGH, (died in 1890).
            - RÁJKUMÁRÍ RATAN KUAR, [(*grand-daughter*, at present in possession (1892)].
        - RÁNÍ SANET KUAR, (*wife*).

Four miles to the west of Tikari town is the important village of Konch, where there is an ancient brick temple which is lighted by a tall opening in front formed by overlapping courses of bricks after the fashion of the great temple at Bodh Gayá. This temple, however, is Brahmanical, as it enshrines a *lingam* of Śiva Kocheśvara. Externally it differs from the two great temples at Náland́á and Bodh Gayá, in having its sides curved instead of being in straight lines from top to bottom. It differs also in its style of ornamentation, as there are no external niches, and consequently no enshrined figures. The exterior is instead covered with a carved pattern, now partly concealed by plaster. The hall contains numerous sculptures, the most curious of which are those known as the *Das Avatár*, or ten incarnations of Vishnu. In this group the usual Buddha incarnation appears to have been intentionally omitted or, at least, placed in a position which would escape observation. To the east of the temple is a large sheet of water, with brick-covered mounds on all sides, together with two ruined temples. The village to the south of the lake and great temple also possess several sculptures, of which the best are a Vishnu and a seated Buddha. All these Konch remains are attributed by tradition to a Kol Rájá named Duraj. For further information regarding these interesting ruins, the reader is referred to the Reports of the Archæological Survey of India, especially Vol. VIII, pp. 54 and ff., and Vol. XVI, pp. 52 & ff.

Six miles north of Tikari is the village of Kespá, where there are numerous fragments of ancient stone buildings and a famous temple of the Hindu goddess Tárá Deví. The image in the temple, which is carefully kept hidden under a yellow sheet, is, however, believed to be really a male, Buddhist, statue. Páibighá, Belá (with a police-outpost, a police force of 1 head-constable and 4 constables, and a railway station), Ántí, and Maú, are important markets in the Tikari police jurisdiction. Other large villages are Ūr, Nimsar, Kuráp, Kábar, and Sáñrá. Páibighá contains a number of stone pillars which must have once belonged to a temple in honour of Śiva. They are now set up right in front of the village; besides these there are some remains of statues. At Belá there are several remains, about a mile and-a-half to the east of the inspection bungalow. They consist principally of fragments of various statues, mostly Brahmanical, but some are Buddhist ones. In the vicinity are some temples, none of any great antiquity, one of which contains a statue of the goddess Kálí in black stone. Utrain and Pálí are two villages, owned by Government, and situated to the west of the crossing of the river Morhar, about three miles south of Tikari. They contain several mounds of ruins covered with broken bricks and stone figures, and with fragments of architecture. These include the ruins of at least two temples, and a large *argha* or lower half of a *lingam*, 3 feet 10½ inches square. There are also the remains of an old fort, locally known as

Himmat Khán's *gaṛh.* The Barábar hills, which fall within the boundaries of the Belá police outpost, will be found described under the head of the Jahanabad subdivision.

SHERGHATI (more accurately Sherghâṭí), also known as Shaharghâṭí, and formerly the head-quarters of a subdivision of the same name, is situated at the point where the Grand Trunk Road crosses the Morhar on two handsome bridges, in N. latitude 24° 33′ 24″ and E. longitude 84° 50′ 28″. Before the East Indian Railway was extended to Patna, the position of this town on the Grand Trunk Road rendered it a very important place. The remains of the European residences and the number of monuments in the cemetery afford proofs of this. There are still to be found here the descendants of skilled artisans, workers in brass, wood, and iron; but the town is now retrograding. The subdivision was broken up in 1871, and with the exception of an occasional subordinate in the Public Works Department, there are at the present time no European residents. When this town formed part of the district of Rámgaṛh, it was a centre of crime, which led to the appointment of a special Joint-Magistrate in 1814. It is now the head-quarters of a police-station with a force of 1 sub-inspector, 1 head-constable, and 12 constables. The population of the police jurisdiction, according to the census of 1891, is 154,229, of whom 73,297 are males and 80,932 are females. There is an interesting old fort here, said to have been built by the Kol Rájás.

ḌOBHÍ, lies on the Grand Trunk Road between Barachati and Sherghati, about seven miles east of the latter town. There is an inspection-bungalow here, and travellers between Gaya and Sherghati usually go round by this village. Here also is a road police post, for patrolling the Grand Trunk Road, and keeping it open for travellers.

Six miles north-west of Sherghati is the large bazar and police-outpost (with 1 head-constable and 3 constables) of GURUÁ, which has on its south side a tank, locally famous for its white lotuses, and on its east a modern temple and tank dedicated to the sun, the former of which is now falling into disrepair. Two miles west of Guruá a spring issues from the earth at a place called Búṛhá or Ḍúbhá, and is the site of a fair held at the full moon of the month of Kártik. About two miles further south is the village of Guneri, the ancient *Śri Guṇacharita*, formerly the site of a Buddhist monastery; there are also the ruins of several Śiva temples. At Chillor, on the left bank of the Morhar, about three miles east of Guruá, there are said to be some interesting remains.

Eighteen miles south-west of Sherghati lies the important trade centre of Ránígaṇj, where a market is held once a week. Lac, frankincense, sesamum, clarified butter, and wood are the principal commodities sold. There are also important lac-factories both here and in the neighbouring town of Imámgañj. Other important marts in the Sherghati police jurisdiction are Náráyanpur, Roshangañj, Ámas, and Amárut. Eight miles south of the last-named village, at Birátpur, there are a tank and a temple dedicated to Kauleswarí Deví, which, however, owing to their inaccessible position on a steep hill, are not much visited. The Páṇḍava heroes of the Mahábhárata are said to have concealed themselves for a year in this fortress, the scenery of which is very beautiful. Other important villages in the jurisdiction of this police-station are Maigrá and Hardawan. There are police-outposts at Guruá, Imámgañj (with 1 sub-inspector and 4 constables), and Dumariá (with 1 head-constable and 3 constables).

Atari (more properly Antrí), to the north-east of Gaya, in N. latitude 24° 55′ 5″ and E. longitude 85° 17′ 40″, has a police-station with a force consisting of 1 sub-inspector, 1 head-constable, and 9 constables. The population is 123,671, of whom 61,031 are males and 62,640 females. Atari gives its name to the police jurisdiction, but the police-station is situated five miles to the west, at the village of Ṭaṭuá, on the right bank of the river Paimár. It has under it an independent police-outpost at Khizr Sarái with a force of 1 sub-inspector and 4 constables, whose jurisdiction swarms with members of the criminal classes. Three miles north of the Atari (Ṭaṭuá) station is the hill of Pattharkaṭṭí, where there is a colony of artistic stone-cutters. These men are Brahmans, whose ancestors are said to have come from Jaipur to build the Vishnupad temple at Gaya. They only marry amongst themselves. Five miles north-west of this place we come to the village of Mírápur Naderá, where the ruins of a number of Hindu temples have been converted into mosques. The chief object of interest is an old *dargáh* about half a mile east of the village, ascribed to Sayyad Ahmad Sháh, a local saint. In the *dargáh* is a tree to which females for miles around come to tie *chillás* with the object of obtaining children. The *chillá* consists of a small piece of the dress of the wearer, which must be torn and tied to one of the branches of the tree. The woman tying the *chillá* must visit the spot quite alone and at night. About ten miles west of Ṭaṭuá, in the midst of the hills, there is a chalk-min at Araí. The sacred hot springs of Tapoban, visited by Hiuen Tsiang, are two miles south-west of Araí, and are the site of a fair held on the Makara Sankránti, the passage of the sun from Sagittarius to Capricornus. About a mile and three quarters north of Tapoban is the village of Jeṭhian, which has been identified by General Cunningham with the *Yashṭívana* or bamboo forest also visited by the pilgrim, when journeying from Bakraur, *viá* Kuṛkihár, to Rájgir. After leaving Yashṭívana he came to the *Buddhavana* (Buddha's forest), the modern Budhain, four miles north of Jeṭhian. Thence he descended into the Rájgir valley. Jeṭhian is situated in a narrow fertile continuation of the Rájgir valley between two ranges of hills running north-east and south-west, which contains many objects of interest. The principal is the Rájá Piṇḍá, on the west face of the eastern range, about two miles from Jeṭhian village. It is situated half-way up the steep scarp of the hill, and is approached by a very ancient built road, which runs, apparently for some miles, at a fairly uniform level of about five hundred feet above the valley. The road terminates in the *piṇḍá*, which is a large built stone platform at the foot of a steep precipice and commands a magnificent view. A hundred yards south a continuation of the same road, built along the face of the precipice, leads to a fine cave, the exploration of which, owing to the stench caused by thousands of pigeons, is very difficult. Another place of interest is the shrine of Jangalo Bíbí, a Musalmán saint, situated on the summit of a precipitous and thorny hill at the north-west corner of the valley. The saint is worshipped impartially both by Musalmáns and Hindus. Pilgrims climb to the shrine with great difficulty, worship and eat pottage (*khichrí*) cooked in the water of a perennial reservoir which is close by. It is believed that this act of devotion saves the worshipper from being born as a dog at his next birth. A less important shrine on a hill to the east of Jeṭhian is that of Sahodará Ráni, about whom the writer could collect no traditions.

The other important villages in this jurisdiction are Sarbahidá, Hemárá, Maksúdpur (the head-quarters of Rájá Rameshwar Prasád Náráyan Singh), Sioñtar, Sársú, Kajúr, Riolá, Básar, Kuṛkíhár (see head-quarters thana) and Púrá.

Barachati (or more accurately Báráchaṭṭí) lies nearly twenty miles south of Gaya, on the Grand Trunk Road in N. latitude 24° 30′ 10″ and E. longitude 84° 50′ 28.″ It has a local police force consisting of 1 sub-inspector, 2 head-constables, and 10 constables. There is an inspection-bungalow at Kahuḍág, two miles to the east. The neighbourhood was formerly famous for its shooting, and even of late years tigers have been seen in the neighbourhood. There are road police posts at Salaiyá and Bhaluá to keep the Grand Trunk Road open for travellers. The population of the jurisdiction is 109,488, of whom 53,666 are males and 55,822 are females.

About sixteen miles north-east of Barachati, west of the river Ḍáḍhar, is the police-outpost of Fat'hpur (with 1 sub-inspector and 4 constables), formerly inhabited by wealthy Khattrís, who built a fort, but they are now no longer prosperous. A short distance to the south-east is a temple of Sáṇḍeśwara Mahádeva, of which the image is said to be very ancient. A fair is held here at the festival of the Śivarátri on the 14th of the dark half of the month of Mágh. Half-way between Barachati and Fat'hpur on the right bank of the Muháná river is the small village of Lakhaipur, where there is a police-outpost (with 1 head-constable and 4 constables). The country here is very wild, and much resorted to for sport. An ancient fort here contains a sacred well, now dry, in which a Kol queen and her handmaidens are said to have drowned themselves to preserve their honour, when the stronghold was conquered by the troops of the Tikari Ráj.

Other important villages in the Barachati jurisdiction are Bindá (principally inhabited by Káyasths), Bairiyá, Sarwáñ, and Ḍangrá. The last two are markets, and are much infested by apes.

NAWÁDAH SUBDIVISION.

Nawádah (more properly Nawádá or Nau-abádá) is situated on both sides of the Khurí river, in N. latitude 24° 52′ 42″ and E. longitude 85° 35′ 1″, in the centre of the subdivision of which it is the head-quarters. The portion of the village on the left bank is the older, and is called Ḍíh; that on the right bank is modern, and contains the public offices and a *sarái* or hostel. It has a police-station with a force consisting of 1 sub-inspector, 2 head-constables, and 14 constables. The population is under 5,000; but as almost the whole trade of the neighbourhood must pass through this place, it should rise in importance. The population of the police jurisdiction is 282,923, of whom 138,266 are males and 144,657 females. That of the subdivision is 439,565, of whom 215,320 are males and 224,245 are females. The only metalled roads in the subdivision are the Bihár and Rajauli road, which runs north and south and passes through the town, and the road to Gaya. During the famine of 1873-74 this latter road was extended as an unmetalled road east to the confines of the subdivision, where it joins a road in the adjoining district, and thus forms a direct route from Monghyr to Gaya. Another important mart, Wárisalíganj, was also connected with Nawádah during the famine year.

Nawádah has but little historical interest. Before its acquisition by the Company it was ruled by the nearly independent Rájás of Hasuá. After the settlement, and previously to the creation of the subdivision in 1845, the whole neighbourhood was in great disorder. The only police-station was at this place, and the entire force for the subdivision consisted of a *darogá*, two or three subordinate officers, and about twenty constables.

About two miles north of Nawádah, to the west of the public road, there is a handsome Jain temple and tank. The temple was built by Babus Lachhmípat and Dhanpat Singh, the well-known bankers of Murshidabad. Four miles to the north-east, on the left bank of the river Sakrí, lies the important mart of Kádirgañj, where there was formerly a considerable trade in *tasar* silk.

Six miles north-east of Kádirgañj, on the right bank of the river Sakri, is situated the village of WÁRISALÍGAÑJ or WORSELEYGANJ, which is said by some to have been founded by, and named after, a Mr. Worseley, a former Deputy Magistrate of Nawádah. Really it was founded by one Wáris Alí Khán, a member of the family of the well-known Kámdár Khán. It forms the head-quarters of a police-outpost (with a force of 1 head-constable and 4 constables), and has a large trade in linseed and in saltpetre. In the vicinity are the important villages of Sámbe, Kochgáoñ, Makanpur, Samái, and Kuṭarí.

Eight miles west of Nawádah, on the Gaya road, near the river Tilaiyá, lies the important town of HASUÁ, where there is also an independent police-outpost with a force of 1 sub-inspector and 4 constables. It has a considerable reputation for the ornamental pottery of good quality, which is here manufactured. It is also of historical interest as having once been the head-quarters of the well-known Kámdár Khán, whose forts are scattered all over the Nawádah sub-division.

Six miles south-west of Hasuá, at Sítámaṛhí, a curious isolated boulder has been hollowed to form a small chamber about 16 feet long by 11 wide. The interior is highly polished, and tradition makes it the residence of Sítá during her exile, and relates that it was here that her son Lava was born. It was in the wide high level ground near this boulder that Lava and Kuśa are said to have fought with Ráma's army. About a mile to the east is a group of rocky hills, which are covered with ruins. On one of the hills, near the village of Rasúlpúrá, is the tomb of a local saint named Shekh Muḥammad. Judging from the style of the dome, the building dates from a very early period, and it no doubt occupies the site of some older Hindu shrine. A mile to the north-east of Sítámaṛhí is the village Bárat, where the poet and saint Válmíki is said to have lived when Sítá was sent into exile. It was at his order that Viśvakarman, the architect of the gods, constructed the rock cave for her. At present, the only object of notice at this place is an old mud fort standing on a high mound.

Two miles south of Nawádah is the large village of Barew, with the ruins of one of Kámdár Khán's forts, and an old mosque in good condition; and six miles further east, on the direct pilgrim road to Baijnáth, the important market of Gobindpur, with a police-outpost (with 1 head-constable and 4 constables). South-west of Gobindpur, at a distance of six miles, near the village of Ektárá, the waterfall of Kakolaṭ is situated at one of the most beautiful spots in the district. At its foot a large fair is held at the Mekh Sankránti, the passage of the sun from Aries to Taurus. About five miles north-west of Gobindpur the village of Siúr is remarkable for some very large mounds of ruins, as yet unexplored.

The important village of Akbarpur, ten miles south of Nawádah, contains a monastery of the Nánhakpanthí sect.

RAJAULI (more accurately Rajaulí) is situated almost in the extreme south-east of the district, in N. latitude 24° 39′ and E. longitude 85° 32′ 25″, on the left bank of the Dhanárjay river. It is an important mart, with a population of over 5,000 souls. It is connected with Bihár town by a metalled road passing through Nawádah, from which it is distant eighteen miles due south. It is the head-quarters of a police-station, with a staff of 1 sub-inspector, 1 head-constable, and 10 constables. The population of the police jurisdiction is 74,859, of whom 36,228 are males and 38,631 females. It has also a branch monastery of the Akbarpur institution, and a Musalmán charitable endowment, called the *Sháh Sáhib kí takiyá*. The latter has a sacred fire (*dhúí*), said to have been lit three hundred years ago by fire brought from Mecca.

Six miles south of Rajauli, in the midst of wild hills, lies the village of Síngar, near which is a valuable talc-mine. There are other talc-mines more to the east, in the heart of the jungles, which are worked with varying profit.

Three miles north-west of Rajauli is the village of Amáwáñ, which is inhabited by both Hindus and Musalmáns. It is remarkable for the number of its inhabitants (especially Káyasths and Musalmáns) who have taken service elsewhere. South of the village there is a ruined fort and a tank. The town also possesses a Nánhakshábí monastery.

According to tradition, the whole of the jurisdiction of Rajauli police-station is sacred ground. Seven miles south-east of Rajauli, in the hills, is Dubáur (Durvásaḥpura), where dwelt the irascible but holy Durvásas, the son of Atri and Anasúyá, who cursed Śakuntalá for keeping him waiting at her door, and so caused the separation between her and Dushyanta. He even cursed Indra for treating with disrespect a garland which the sage presented to him. Krishṇa, also, we are told, died according to the imprecation of Durvásas, because on one occasion, when hospitably entertaining the holy man, he omitted to wipe the fragments of food from his feet. Four miles north-east of Rajauli is a pretty hill, called Lomasgir (Lomaśa-giri), with a cave said to have been the residence of another sage, named Lomaśa, who may have been the same as the saint-king Loma-páda. Síngar (Śṛiṅga-giri) was the home of the saint Ṛishya-Śṛiṅga. He was brought up in the forest and never saw another human being except his father till he was verging upon manhood. At this time there came a great drought in the neighbouring country of Aṅga or Monghyr, and the king, Loma-páda, was advised by his Brahmans to send for the youth Ṛishya-Śṛiṅga, who should marry his daughter Śántá and be the means of obtaining rain. This was done. The youthful saint married Śántá, and rain came.

This Śántá was the adopted daughter of Loma-páda, her real father being Daśaratha, and it was Ṛishya-Śṛiṅga who performed that sacrifice for Daśaratha which brought about the birth of Ráma.

Dubáur is, according to some, the birthplace of the famous Goálá hero Lorik, whose deeds are recited at the present day, by men of that caste, in songs of interminable length. The following account of the legend is based upon that given in Volume VIII of the Reports of the Archæological Survey of India, but is different in some particulars :—

Lorik was the son of a Goálá named Buṛhkubbhá, and was born at Dubáur (others say a place called Gaurághâṭ). He was married to a girl in the village of Baurí (others say Agaurí, near Rajauli), three miles south-east of Rajauli, and a large hollowed stone is shown there to the present day, in which he used to mix his *bhâng*. A huge rock, which he is said to have cleft in two with his sword, is also there displayed to the faithful. Although married, his wife, Mánjar, was not of age, and she had not yet come to live with him.

There was a man of Dubáur, named Siodhar, who was cursed by the goddess Parvati to lose all desire. He had been married in his infancy, before the curse, and in due course, when his wife Chandáin (who was daughter of the local Rájá) became of age, he brought her to his home ; but as all desire had been destroyed in him, his wife not only despised him, but formed an attachment with Lorik, her fellow-villager, and eloped with him and all her jewellery into the Patna district. Siodhar pursued and overtook them, but was defeated by Lorik in fight, and the latter and Chandáin then went leisurely on. On the road, near Bárágáoñ (the ancient Nálanda) in the Patna district, at a place where there is now a large headless statue, they met the king of the *juárís* or gamblers, named Mahápatiyá, a Dosádh by caste, from Juáphar in the same district. Lorik and he sat down and gambled till the former had lost everything he had, including Chandáin. Mahápatiyá now got up to seize her, but she said, "I have indeed been staked and lost, but the jewels on my person were not staked, so play one game more with the jewels for a stake." The gambler sat down to play, and Chandáin, by a very indecent stratagem, distracting his attention, he lost back to Lorik, not only all that he had previously won from him, but also all that he had himself. At Chandáin's instigation Lorik then attacked Mahápatiyá, who had looked on her with lustful eyes. Lorik took his sword, weighing two maunds, and with one stroke sent the gambler's head flying to Juáphar, while his body fell where he was seated, and both have since been turned into stone, and remain as a witness there to this day.

Lorik and Chandáin journeyed on towards Hardí, near Munger (Monghyr), where they fought with and defeated the Rájá of that country. Other authorities place Hardí in the North-Western Provinces, near Baliá. The expelled Rájá sued for aid at the Court of Kalinga, and succeeded with his help in capturing Lorik, who was forthwith placed in a cell, with his hands and feet stretched out to their fullest extent and nailed down to the floor. A heavy load was also placed on his chest, and in this state he lay for a long time, till, at last, through the favour of the goddess Durgá, he escaped from confinement. He again fought with and defeated the Rájá, reconquered Hardí, and was reunited with Chandáin. Here they had a son born, and lived a long time, but at last a desire to revisit their native country arose in their hearts.

In the meantime, Mánjar, Lorik's legitimate wife, had grown up to be a handsome woman, still living with her sister Lurkí, in her father's house, at Baurí, and in great distress. Lorik had also a foster-brother, Sauñrú, who, being an orphan, had been brought up by Lorik's father as a son. He lived near Baurí, at a village which, from the circumstance of his having been brought up as an adopted son, "*pálak*," was called Pálí. His wife's name was Satmanáin. This Sauñrú had, during Lorik's absence, been attacked by the Kols, and all his cattle and property had been plundered.

Sauñrú had fought for seven days with the Kols, but as he was apparently invulnerable, they could not at first beat him. Finally a traitor informed them that he was vulnerable only in the heel,* and they wounded him there, and, crying Rám, Rám,. he gave up the ghost. His wife Satmanáin became *satí* for him, and he left only a son, Abhorí, whose family, like that of Mánjar, fell into great distress.

Lorik and Chandáin having started from Hardí, arrived at Pálí laden with wealth, and gave out that a Rájá from a distant country had arrived. Time had so changed him that no one recognized him, and he determined to ascertain whether his wife had been faithful to him during his absence. Accordingly, when he had ascertained that his wife was among the women who came daily to sell milk in his camp, and had recognised her, though she failed to recognise him, he caused a *dhotí* (or loin-cloth) to be placed across the entrance to his camp, so that no one could come in without striding across it. Next morning, when the women came, he instructed Chandáin to call them in quick, judging that if his wife, in her hurry, should step across the *dhotí*, and thus show that she was not particular in a trifling matter, she was not likely to have been particularly careful as to her virtue. Mánjar, hurried by Chandáin, came on fast till she came to the *dhotí*, and though others stepped over it, she stood still, and requested that it might be removed. Lorik was pleased at this, and when she had disposed of her milk and

* A curious coincidence with the legend of Achilles.

wanted payment, instead of giving her the usual payment in rice, he filled her basket with jewels and covered them with the grain, so that she unsuspectingly took them home. Her sister, Lurkí, on emptying the basket, saw the wealth below, and surmising that she had obtained it at the price of her honour, taxed her with it. Mánjar denied all knowledge of the jewels, and the girls agreed to go next day together, so as to have the suspicion cleared off. Meanwhile, Sauñrú's son, Abhorí, hearing of the scandal against his aunt, took up arms to attack Lorik, not knowing that he was Mánjar's husband. The two women went as agreed. Lurkí recognized Lorik, and the mystery was cleared up to the satisfaction of every one concerned. Lorik got a scolding, but was allowed to keep on Chandáin as well as his wife. On the other hand, Abhorí, not having any knowledge of these transactions, and finding Lurkí and Mánjar both absent from home, furiously attacked Lorik, and after a long and terrible fight was in the act of taking his life, when Lurkí and Mánjar rushed up, and explained matters. Thereupon there were great rejoicings, and all settled down happily.

Lorik ruled his subjects with justice, and so encouraged agriculture, that the barren land round Rajauli was turned into a cultivated plain, and birds, beasts and insects lost all secure resting places. So they went and complained to Indra, who, taking counsel with Durgá, said that Lorik was so blameless in his private life, that he was beyond the power of harm, and could not be touched, unless he committed some crime. To entice him into crime, Durgá assumed the form of his mistress, and went to him with his food, which was the usual custom of Chandáin. Lorik, ignorant of the trap laid for him, and not noticing that she cast no shadow, and was therefore not a mortal, became inflamed by the beauty of his supposed mistress, who on this day seemed more beautiful than ever, and neglecting his food, made amorous advances to her. Hardly had he touched her, when Durgá, knowing that his invulnerability was lost, administered such a slap to him, that his face was twisted completely round. She then disappeared, and, overcome with grief and shame, Lorik determined to go and die at the holy city of Banáras. His relatives, who all loved him too well to lose him, followed him thither, and now all, having been turned into stone, sleep the sleep of magic at the Maníkárniká *ghát̤* in that city.

Pakribarwan (more accurately Pakrí Baráñwáñ) is a police-station and market of some importance. It has a police force of 1 sub-inspector, 1 head-constable, and 9 constables. The population of the jurisdiction is 81,783, of whom 40,826 are males and 40,937 are females. About ten miles east of it the pretty valley of Kauwá Kol, owned principally by a family of Ṭikaits, is rich in iron ore, which is dug up with very little labour near Pachambá. There was formerly a police-outpost, with a force of 1 head-constable and 4 constables, at the latter place, but it has recently been moved to Kauwá Kol. The principal village in the jurisdiction of this police-station is Budhaulí, where there is a wealthy Hindu monastery with its *mahanth*, or abbot. *Ghí* is exported. The village of Roh, in the jurisdiction of this police-station, possesses a mound with several statues and the remains of buildings. Close by is an old well, into which an inscribed slab found here is said to have been thrown.

The famous ruins of Rájgir are situated about twelve miles to the north-west of Nawádah, and are just beyond the border, in the district of Patna. The Báwan Gangá defile and stream of Rájgir, however, debouch in Gaya district, in the jurisdiction of Nawádah police-station. The following legend regarding it, taken from the eighth volume of the Reports of the Archæological Survey of India, will be found interesting:—

There was a Dosádh living in Rájgir, whose daughter used to take the household pigs out in the field to feed. It happened that as she was so engaged on the day of the full moon of a certain great festival, she saw a Bráhman walking on very rapidly. On questioning him, he replied he was going to bathe in the Ganges on the full moon. The girl replied:—"You can't possibly reach the Ganges in time; but if you believe me, and your mind be full of faith, this is the exact moment of the full moon, and here is a pool (in which her pigs were wallowing); dip into it and you will realise the full fruits of bathing in the Ganges at this auspicious moment." The Bráhman did as desired, and when he was in the pool, she said—"Now is the exact moment; dive in and see what you get." He did so, and found the bottom full of valuable gems, of which he clutched a handful and came up. "Dive again," said the girl. He dived again, and found only mud at the bottom. "You see," said the girl, "that I told you only the truth, when I said you will be too late if you go to the Ganges, for at the moment of your first diving the moon was at its exact full, and you got your reward." The Bráhman was astonished, and, seeing her as lovely as she was wise, proposed marriage. She referred him to her father, who refused, saying he could not presume to ally his daughter of low caste to a high caste Bráhman. The Bráhman thereupon threatened to kill himself, and the Dosádh, fearful of incurring the guilt of a Brahmacide, consented after consulting his friends; the marriage was duly solemnised, and the girl then taught her husband to ask no dowry of her father except a particular cow, a particular pig, and a particular parrot. The Dosádh, on bidding his daughter good-bye and God-speed when they were departing, desired his son-in-law to ask for any gift he chose. The Bráhman refused, but being pressed, he bound the Dosádh by a promise to grant his request, and then asked for the pig, the cow, and the parrot, as he had been taught. The Dosádh was taken aback, but, bound by his promise, was obliged to give them up. With these the bridegroom and his bride departed. The parrot was an extraordinary one, as he used to go daily to Indra's court and bring the news of what took place there to his mistress; the pig was the leader of all the pigs in the country; and the cow was no other than the famous "Surabhi," or Cow of Plenty. One day the parrot told his mistress that Indra had given orders that, during the approaching rainy season, it should rain nowhere in the district except on the sterile hills and stony valleys of Rájgir. The girl, hearing this, immediately called her pig and directed him to dig up the whole of the stony valleys and hill slopes of Rájgir; the pig, with the aid of his subject pigs, did as desired. She then directed her husband to go and scatter paddy in all these dug-up places, explaining the object to him. He did as desired. When it rained, the paddy seed sprouted and the whole of stony Rájgir was full of paddy, while outside not a blade of paddy was to be found, owing to want of rain. It being reported to Indra that within Rájgir enough paddy had been grown to avert famine, he ordered an army of mice and rats to be sent to destroy the crops; but the girl, informed of this order by her parrot, got her husband to procure an army of cats as guard; when it was reported to Indra that this plan of destroying the crop had failed, he directed that when cut, each of the paddy sheaves should produce only 1¼ seer of clean paddy; the girl, told by her parrot of this order, directed her husband to make bundles of only two stalks of paddy, each tied end to end; the order of Indra having already gone forth and being therefore irrevocable, each bundle consisting of two stalks of paddy produced 1¼ seer of paddy; Indra informed of this, and seeing himself outwitted, ordered a furious storm to blow and scatter all the paddy which had been threshed out ready for storing; the girl thereupon, aware that no wattle and daub could resist the storm, should she for safety build such to store her paddy in, directed her husband to dig the deep moat now seen in Rájgir round the wall near the foot of the hills; when the storm came, it naturally blew all the paddy down the slopes into these trenches, where it lay snug until the storm had blown over. Thus was the country saved from famine through the talents of this girl, in memory of whom, the pool where her pigs used to wallow in the southern defile at the south gate of the hill-girt city was named Báwan Gangá, or Fifty-two Gangás (see below).

The archæological interest of this subdivision circles round Giriyak, which lies just north of the present boundaries of the district. An account of the ruins at this place is given in the statistical account of Patna.

The following legend about Jarásandha's *baiṭhak* (or sitting platform), which is at Giriyak, may be inserted here. It is taken, with a few alterations, from the eighth volume of the Reports of the Archæological Survey of India:—

When Jarásandha was king, he built the tower on the Giriyak hill as his *baiṭhak*; here he would sit and lave his feet in the waters of the Panchána below. Close to his *baiṭhak* was his garden, which in a year of unusual drought was nearly destroyed. Accordingly, after fruitless efforts to keep it flourishing, he caused it to be proclaimed that he would grant his daughter and half his kingdom to him who should succeed in saving his garden from the effects of the drought by watering it plentifully during a single night with Ganges water.

The chief of the Kahárs, Chandráwaṭ, at once came forward and undertook the task; first he built the great embankment to bring the waters of the Báwan Gangá rivulet to the foot of the hill below the garden, and then began lifting it up to successive stages by means of the common native *cháñr* (swing basket) and ropes. It is necessary here to remark that the Báwan Gangá is considered to be a part of the Ganges and to equal in holiness the united sanctity of Ganges waters from the Báwan Tírthas, or fifty-two places of pilgrimage. The Kahárs who were to labour at the work were provided with cakes of bread and balls of rice; with these for sustenance they (still the hardiest and sturdiest tribe in Magadha) laboured all night and succeeded in watering the garden; but when Jarásandha saw their success, unwilling to ally his daughter to a Kahár, he looked about for means to cheat the chief of his fairly-earned reward. Now the Pípal-tree came forward and offered his services to Jarásandha, proposing to assume the form of a cock and crow, while Járasandha was to urge the Kahárs to hasten the operations, as the garden was not yet sufficiently watered.

This ruse succeeded completely. The Kahárs, hearing the cock crow simultaneously with Jarásandha's urging them to hasten, concluded that all was lost, as the garden had not been, they thought, sufficiently watered before the crowing of the cock, the signal for morning; so, afraid of their lives for their presumption in venturing to seek Jarásandha's daughter as the bride of their chief, they all fled and lay exhausted on the banks of the Ganges at Mokámá, where the railway station now is.

When day fairly broke, Jarásandha ordered the Kahárs to be brought that he might give them their wages, for though, he said, they had been unsuccessful in winning his daughter and half his kingdom, they had nevertheless laboured hard and were deserving of some consideration; but not a Kahár was to be found.

At last news reached the Kahárs at Mokámá, and a few came up to receive their wages. Jarásandha gave each man 3½ seers of *anáj* (food-grain), and ever since that period 3½ seers of *anáj* have been the legitimate wages for a day's work to Kahárs. To this day the Kahárs can legally claim, and as a matter of fact actually receive, the value of 3½ seers of food-grain in current coin as a day's wages. Subsequently, thus re-assured that their lives were not in danger, they returned to their villages and lived in peace. The bread cakes and rice balls they had abandoned in their flight from the hill still exist, turned to stone.

Nine miles north-east of Giriyak and about six miles north of Wáris-alíganj, on the river Sakrí, and exactly on the commen boundary of the Patna and Gaya districts, is the village of Daryápur Párbatí. The hill here is identified, with some hesitation, by General Cunningham as the site of the Buddhist Kapotiká or pigeon monastery, visited by Hiuen Tsiang. Párbatí is also called Parávata, which means 'pigeon.' The hill was once filled with wild pigeons, which formed an important food-supply to the neighbourhood in the famine of 1873-74. The whole surface of the hill is literally covered with ruins, probably the remains of "the multitudes of viharas and temples" seen by the Chinese pilgrim. These ruins have been largely dug into for bricks for road making and for building modern houses, and also for treasure which has more than once been found. A *stupa* was built here by Aśoka to commemorate one of the Buddha's miracles. The Buddha changed himself here into a pigeon for the benefit of a fowler and his starving family. When the man went to return thanks to the Buddha for his opportune relief, he was duly converted, and, repenting of his faults, became a new man, and eventually obtained the dignity of *Arhat*. Exactly in the middle of the hill to the south stood the famous temple of Avalokiteśvara, with an image of the Bodhisattwa in sandalwood. He bore a lotus in his hand, and over his head was an image of the Buddha. The story goes that a King of Ceylon once, when bathing in the sea, saw, as if in a mirror, not a reflection of his own body, but the statue of Avalokit-eśvara standing on the top of a small hill surrounded with palm trees in the kingdom of Magadha. He accordingly sought for it, and finding it on the hill of the pigeon monastery, built a *vihára* on the spot. Other kings subsequently followed his example, until the whole hill was covered with temples. The site of the temple is now occupied by a small Musalmán *dargáh* or shrine, built of stones taken from the ruins. Tradition says that an old Hindu *fakír* once lived here, when a corpse came floating down the river Sakrí. The *fakír* dreamed that the corpse told him that its name was Chánd Hájí, and that it wanted a decent burial in a grave to be dug on a spot, near the south-east end of the hill, which he described. As a reward he promised the sovereignty of the district to the *fakír*. The *fakír* did as directed, and became king afterwards. The *dargáh* that now stands was the one built by him. Chánd Hájí, or Chánd Saudágar, is a saint of wide celebrity in Bengal. Many are the spots where this benevolent saint is said to have put silver and gold vessels, &c., for the use of travellers. A traveller on arriving at one of these fortunate spots, which was generally either a well or the bank of a tank, had only to make known his wants, when Chánd Saudágar's vessels of gold and silver would float up and allow themselves to be used by the traveller, who had, however, scrupulously to return them when done with. But men are covetous, and at each of these places some unlucky man has been too weak to resist the temptation of appropriating them, and since then the miracle has ceased. Another legend makes Párbatí a place of importance at the time of the war of the Mahábhárata. According to it, when the sacrificial horse of the Páṇḍavas was let loose, Rájá Śánkhadhvaj, of this place, seized it and prepared to fight. Before joining battle, however, he performed a sacrifice. The Rájá's *guru* (or preceptor) demanded that orders should be given for every one to be ready and present at a given spot by a certain hour. The Rájá's son, Suratidhvaj, was newly married, and his bride happened to arrive that very day, and at her entreaty, Suratidhvaj delayed a short time. The *guru* demanded the punishment of the young man, and accordingly he was thrown into a cauldron of boiling oil, but he came out unhurt. The *guru* suspected that the oil was not hot enough, so he heated it much more, and to try the heat, threw in a piece of the husk of a cocoanut; the violence of the heat caused the husk to be thrown up against the *guru's* face, blinding his right eye and burning away the right half of his face. The Rájá's son, it was found, had escaped, because he had prayed to Vishṇu, and had held a sacred tulsí leaf in his mouth, when jumping into the cauldron.

Three miles to the south-east of Párbatí is the village of Aphsañr which has been identified with the site of a monastery and *stupa* mentioned by Hiuen Tsiang. The Buddha is said to have preached for seven days here in favour of the god Brahma. There are several remains here, both Buddhist and Brahmanical.

Párbatí and Aphsañr are indissolubly connected with the legend of Kunwar Bijai Mall, which forms the theme of a long poem sung by men of the *Telí* caste all over South Bihár. The song has been printed in full and translated by the writer in the Journal of the Asiatic Society of Bengal, and the following is a condensed abstract of a version of the story given in the eighth volume of the Reports of the Archæological Survey of India:—

Kuñwar Bijai Mall used to live in Jhunjhunwá Gaṛh, a place which the writer has not been able to identify. He came to Párbatí to be married to Báwan Subah's daughter, and was accompanied by his father and his elder brothers, being himself a child. Báwan Subah treacherously seized his father and brothers, and put them into prison. Kuñwar Bijai Mall's horse, however, fled with his rider and carried him back safe to Jhunjhunwá Gaṛh. Here he grew up in ignorance of the fate of his father and brothers, and there being no male relatives to avenge his wrongs, his female relatives, of whom his sister-in-law was chief, kept him in this condition, lest he should rashly venture to fight and lose his life. This sister-in-law, named Sonmatí Ráni, took great care of him, had him taught all arts, and intended, when he should grow up, to live with him as his wife. When Bijai Mall did grow up, he wanted bows and arrows and a *gulí ḍaṇḍá*, or tipcat and stick, to play with. Sonmatí Ráni gave him the ordinary wooden ones, but he broke them, and wanted stronger ones. Finally he had made for his special use an iron *ḍaṇḍá* of 84 maunds weight and an iron *gulí* of 80 maunds. These he took and went to play with his companions, but on their refusing on the ground that they could not use his *ḍaṇḍá*, it was agreed that each should use his own *ḍaṇḍá* and *gulí*. When Bijai Mall's turn came, he hit his iron *gulí* with such force that it flew to Gaṛh Párbatí, and smashed in a part of Báwan Subah's palace. His companions searched for the *gulí* for seven days, but, not finding it, they came disgusted to Kuñwar Bijai Mall, and asked him why, when he was so strong, he did not go and release his father and brothers from confinement. Accordingly, he went to his sister-in-law, and demanded to be told the circumstances of their confinement; she long tried to evade his questions, but finding him persist, she went and adorned herself superbly, and radiant with gems and beauty, approached him; he asked her why she had adorned herself; she said—"Your brothers and father went west to fight, and I expect them back to-night." This he would not believe, but, drawing his sword, threatened to kill her; then she told him the whole truth. The groom of the horse, Jhingná Khawás, was called and confirmed her story, and Bijai Mall ordered the horse and arms to be brought and prepared to go. Sonmatí Ráni begged him to eat before starting; he sat down and finished his supper; then she besought him to lie down and rest for a while; he did so and fell asleep; she thereupon went and laid herself beside him. On waking and seeing her, he rejected her advances, saying—"I consider you as my mother. Be not uneasy for me. I will go and rescue your husband and my father in four days." She then left him, and he went to Gaṛh Párbatí.

At that time a covered passage led from the palace of Báwan Subah to the tank at Aphsañr. Kuñwar Bijai Mall, on arriving, alighted near that tank; a female servant of Báwan Subah's daughter soon arrived at the tank to carry water. Seeing him there, she asked him who he was, and how he dared to walk about near that tank. This led to hot words between them, and the young man having very ungallantly seized the damsel and torn her clothes, she beat a hasty retreat, and went and informed her mistress, Ráni Tilko. Meanwhile Ráni Tilko, the wife of Kuñwar Bijai Mall, had seen the young man from the roof of her house, and had taken a fancy to him, and when the maid complained of his conduct, she pacified her and desired her not to let her father hear of it. She then went with her companions, all dressed exactly like her, to the tank on pretence of bathing, but really to see the audacious young man. On reaching the place, she saw him still there, and went up to him to ask him his name, and whence he came. On hearing his name she immediately covered her face, as she saw she had met her husband, and on being asked in her turn who she was, her reply showed Kuñwar Bijai Mall that he had met his wife. There was then a very tender scene between them, she beseeching him to take her and fly, and he refusing to run away with her like a thief, but expressing his determination to win her with his sword. Tilko Ráni returned sorrowful to her apartments, and prayed for her husband's success against her father. Kuñwar Bijai Mall, on the other hand, went to the prison where his father and brothers were confined; but finding the walls and gate of adamant (*bajr*), he despaired. Here his horse, seeing his grief, came forward and smashed in the gates, so that he got in and released the prisoners. He then went and pillaged the favourite *bazár* of Báwan Subah. News of these events having now reached the latter, he sent the chief of his forces to fight Kuñwar Bijai Mall, and on his defeat, he sent his son with fresh troops, which, however, shared the same fate. Báwan Subah then went out himself. Long the battle raged, Kuñwar Bijai Mall not wishing to kill, but to capture his enemy; in this he at last succeeded, and he cut off one of Báwan Subah's hands, and put out one eye of his son. He then set them free, and demanded that his wife, Báwan Subah's daughter, should be sent to his house with due pomp and ceremony, as she was now of age. There was no alternative for Báwan Subah but to comply. He did so, and Kuñwar Bijai Mall returned to his own house accompanied by his brother, Sonmatí Ráni's husband, his father, and his own wife.

It may be added that the ruins round Chánd Saudágar's *dargáh* at Párbatí are now known as Báwan Subah's palace, while two other mounds, which have been dug into for treasure, are known as his *baiṭhak*, or sitting room, and his *kachahrí* respectively.

JAHANABAD SUBDIVISION.

JAHANABAD (more accurately Jahánábád), the head-quarters of the subdivision, is situated in N. latitude 25° 13′ 10″ and E. longitude 85° 2′ 10″, on the Patna branch road, 31 miles due north of Gaya, and rather more than half-way to Patna. The subdivision contains a population of 393,817 persons, of whom 195,886 are males and 197,931 females. The local police consists of 1 sub-inspector, 2 head-constables, and 14 constables. The population of the police jurisdiction is 278,895, of whom 139,118 are males and 139,777 are females. Dr. Buchanan-Hamilton states that in his time the town contained about 700 houses, and that, besides the cloth factory, there was also a native agency for the manufacture of saltpetre. It was once famous for its weaving industry, the cloth manufactured being remarkable for its fineness. This trade attracted numbers of *Khattris*, whose families are still settled in the town, but the trade has entirely disappeared, and the richest inhabitants are now *Telis*. At the confluence of the Jamuná and Dardhá there is a handsome temple, where a fair is held on the full moon of Kátik.

Lying as it does on the direct road midway between Patna and Gaya, Jahanabad has continued to increase in size and importance, though the old cloth trade has dwindled away. Three brick houses, one of which is said to have been built by the Dutch, are all that remain of what was once a flourishing trade. About 1760, when a central cloth-factory of the East India Company was established in Patna, Jahanabad formed one of the eight smaller factories connected with that town. The system adopted for the payment of wages was one of advances; and the weavers worked off their advances by supplying country cloth of different degrees of fineness at fixed rates. Dr. Buchanan-Hamilton found the Jahanabad factory thriving, and mentions the introduction of a system by a late manager of the factory, by which advances were obviated. Each of the 2,200 weavers attached to the factory, who received 4*s*., engaged to work for the Company alone, and was paid on the presentation of the cloth, according to its quality. Soon after this the factory must have languished, and eventually been abolished; for local tradition asserts that the Company's connection with the factory was abandoned seventy years ago. But the industry did not entirely cease at the same time. Up to twenty years ago, a considerable export trade in cotton cloth was carried on in this neighbourhood; but as soon as Manchester entered into competition the trade failed. It was cheaper for the weaver to buy English thread, and for the consumer to buy Manchester piece-goods, than the produce of his own neighbourhood. The town is situated on the right branch of the Morhar river, generally called the Dardhá, and during the floods a large tract of country is laid under water. The usual official buildings are on the south side of the river. The jail, a modern structure, is built with the latest improvements. There is a *ḍák* bungalow between the river and the residence of the subdivisional officer. The dispensary and post-office are on the north side of the stream.

Ṭehṭá, a village on the Patna branch road, about seven miles south of Jahanabad, is chiefly remarkable as being the head-quarters of an opium district. The Sub-Deputy Opium Agent resides generally in Gaya, except during the spring season, when the cultivators bring in their opium to be weighed and packed for transmission to the central factory at Patna. The town also possesses a considerable trade in saltpetre.

Five miles east of Jahanabad lies the village of Káko. Formerly the principal inhabitants were Agarwálás, but they are dying out, and now Musalmáns predominate. At the south-west corner of the village there is a large lake, called the Parihás Pokhar, nearly half a mile long from east to west, by 700 feet broad, which is said to have been dug by Rání Kaikeyí, Ráma's jealous step-mother. There are here three great mounds, each called *gaṛh* or fort, but it seems probable that one at least was a Buddhist monastery. On the north bank of the lake there is a Musalmán *dargáh* or shrine of Bíbí Kamálo. She is said to have been the daughter of the saint whose tomb is on the bank of the Ganges at Jaṭhulí to the east of Patna. Her sister's husband was the holy man whose tomb is at Maner, near the junction of the Sone with the Ganges; and lastly, this sister's son is said to be the saint whose shrine is at Bihár in the Patna district. The mosque and tomb probably date from early in the 15th century. Bíbí Kamálo is said to have come to Káko in the time of Raja Kanak and his wife Hansá. The Rájá was a Buddhist, but in spite of his religion he sent some food made of rat's flesh to Bíbí Kamálo. When the dish arrived, the rats came to life, and the holy woman cursed the Rájá. At once the city of Káko was turned upside down, and the Rájá was buried in the ruins. Other stories say that her husband got tired of his life at Káko and wished to return to his native place, leaving his wife behind him. Accordingly he slipped away and walked until nightfall, when he went to sleep. When, however, he woke in the morning he found himself again in his own house at Káko. Nothing daunted, he started off a second and even a third time, but with the same result, owing to his wife's miraculous powers. Bíbí Kamálo is looked upon as a half-mad or inspired woman, and numbers of stories are told of her eccentricity. One of them has become a proverbial saying—*Sárá Káko jal gayá, Bíbí Kamál soi rahíñ*, "When the whole of Káko was being burnt up, Bíbí Kamálo remained sound asleep." Her spirit is believed to haunt the place, and people from all the country round, both Hindus and Musalmáns, come to her shrine to propitiate her. All who are haunted by ghosts, or afflicted with the evil spirits of persons who have died a violent death, come to pray at her shrine, and generally stay from 20 to 40 days. The stone inscription is smeared with oil three times a day by the pilgrims, who afterwards rub their bodies with this oil, and begin talking like mad people. A course of this ointment is said to be very effectual in driving out evil spirits. For further information, the reader is referred to Volume XVI of the Report of the Archæological Survey of India, pages 36 and ff, from which the above account is condensed.

The important marts in this jurisdiction are Shakurábád, Kurthá (with a police-outpost, 1 head-constable and 4 constables), Manjhos, Makhdúmpur (on the Patna-Gaya Railway, an independent police-outpost, with 1 sub-inspector and 4 constables), Bisunganj, Modanganj, and Hulásganj. The last-named town is really a hamlet of village Surajpúrá, 13½ miles east of Jahanabad. It has a police-outpost of 1 head-constable and 4 constables, and a good inspection bungalow on the right bank of the old dried up bed of the river Phálgú. Amongst the larger villages may be mentioned Lakháwar, Súpí, Kachnáwá, Ikkil, Okrí, and Murgáñw. Ghenjan on the river Morhar, a village belonging to Government, has some mounds of ruins and a few statues, two of which bear more or less complete inscriptions of the Buddhist creed. The statues, though plainly Buddhist, are worshipped by the Brahman inhabitants of the village as images of *Śiva Siddheśvara*, a Hindu deity. Six miles south-east is the village of Nerá on the Gaya-Jahanabad road, where there are the remains of a large Śiva temple.

Arwal is situated in N. latitude 25° 14′ 43″ and E. longitude 84° 42′ 32″, on the river Sone, due east of Jahanabad, near the confines of Patna district, and is the head-quarters of a police-station. The population of the police jurisdiction is 114,922, of whom 56,768 are males and 58,154 females. In Dr. Buchanan-Hamilton's time this town was famous for its sugar and paper manufactories, but the latter industry is now almost extinct. The present importance of the village is due to its being the centre of the only indigo concern in the district, and to its position on the Patna Branch Canal. The local police force consists of 1 sub-inspector, 1 head-constable, and 12 constables. The original town of Arwal has been washed into the Sone, and the police-station is now at Badrábád. Close by are the head-quarters of a large zamindari owned by Europeans. The present owners are the Messrs. Solano.

The Kághazí Mahalla or Paper Quarter of Arwal, which was once famous throughout Bihár, rivalling the larger manufactory at Saháran in Shahabad, is now a heap of ruined houses, which still shelter the remains of a numerous population, once busy and prosperous. It used to have a wide market before Serampore paper was ever heard of. As late as 1811 these paper-makers were in easy circumstances, and large quantities of paper were exported both down the Ganges and across Shahabad, Mirzapur, and Banáras into the North-West Provinces. In the village of Sipáh alone 400 families were employed in the manufacture. Of that large number, only 4 remain. There are also two considerable sugar-manufactories. Weeds from the Sone are used for refining, but the best kinds of sugar are not now manufactured here. The home market absorbs nearly all the produce.

About eight miles south of Arwal stands the shrine of Deokuṇḍ (which, however, is just across the border in the Daudnagar tháua), a handsome temple, where a cattle and horse-fair is held on the festival of the Śivarátri. Pondil, a large village of Káyasths eight miles to the south-east, is remarkable for no trees growing within a radius of four miles round it, owing seemingly to the peculiar nature of the soil. Close to Arwal is the village of Sipáh, formerly inhabited by pensioned soldiers, who received grants of land in lieu of pensions. Ten miles to the south-west lies the large village of Ágánúr, which used in former days to be guarded by ramparts and gates, traces of which still remain. It contains a handsome temple and garden dedicated to Śiva.

Other important markets in the Arwal jurisdiction are Kínjar and Telpá. The larger villages, such as Bambhaí, Karpí, Purán, and Narañgá, are principally inhabited by Bábhans.

The other places of interest in this subdivision have been thus described by Mr. Bourdillon* :—Many of the villages in the subdivision of Jahanabad show evidence of former importance. Dharáwat (in the south-east) was the head-quarters of a *tahsildár* under the *subahdár* of Bihár. It contains a fort built on a mud mound, with mud walls of great thickness, and masonry gateways pierced for musketry. Ruins of similar forts exist at Kínjar, on the Punpun, and at Suneré ; Bilkhará, Sisambá, Telpá, and Hulásganj have all a local history of interest." Dharáwat, it may be added, has been identified as the site of the ancient Buddhist monastery of Gunamatí, which was visited by Hiuen Tsiang. The remains are doubtless those which cover the Kunwá hill at this place, and out of which numerous Buddhist statues have been dug up. A few feet from the foot of the hills stretches a fine rectangular piece of water known as the Chandokhar Ṭál, which is fed by a small stream. To the east of the tank is a temple devoted to Śiva and built about the year 1858. Outside is a very fine life-size, twelve-armed statue, named Bhairab. It is really, however, an ancient Buddhist statue of *Bodhisattwa Avalokiteśvara.* According to some, the ancient name of Dharáwat was *Kanchanapura*, and according to others it was *Dharmapurí* or *Dharmáwar.* The legend runs that it had a Rájá named Padumchakra, whose minister was named Bhíkham. Neither of them had a son, and though both were old, they were induced to make a pilgrimage to a saint on the bank of the Ganges, after which the Rájá had a son named Chandrasena, and the minister a son named Bhoránanda. Chandrasena had a fight with his sister's son named Somadatta, whom he slew ; but

* I have taken the liberty of making a few additions to Mr. Bourdillon's remarks, so as to bring them up to date.

after the battle, he found that he could not release the dagger, with which he had done the deed, from his hand. One day, a thirsty calf came towards him, when the Rájá placed a *loṭá* of water before it, which it drank up greedily, and the dagger at once became loose in his grasp. In remembrance of this event, he determined to make a lake, which should extend as far as his horse when let loose should circle round. The minister, apprehensive of the horse making a longer circuit than convenient, selected the present north-east corner of the tank (where there is now a small ruined temple) as the starting point of the horse, turning his head southwards, so that the hills on the south would be the limit of the size of the tank in that direction. The ground thus marked out forms the Chandokhar Ṭál. The next morning the Rájá himself dug out five baskets of earth, and his followers did the same, except one Rájput soldier, who sat with his sword in his hand. When the Rájá asked him why he did not dig out five baskets of earth like the rest, he replied that he was a soldier, and only used to carry arms and letters. On hearing this the Rájá gave him a letter to Bhíkham, king of Lanká or Ceylon, and ordered him to bring back a *láṭ*, or monolith, to place in the middle of the lake. Bhíkham accordingly gave up the pillar, which the soldier carried off; but as he got near Dharáwat the cock crew, and he was therefore obliged to drop it at once at a place now called *Láṭ*, only six miles to the east of Dharáwat, where it still lies. The above is the legend given in the Reports of the Archæological Survey. A slightly different version of the latter portion is given by Mr. Bourdillon, and will be found below.

Mr. Bourdillon continues—

"But the archæological interest of this subdivision centres in the Barábar Hills,* which stand at its south-eastern corner. The highest peak of these hills is crowned by a temple of great antiquity, sacred to Siddheśvara, which contains a *lingam*, said to have been placed there by Bárá Rájá, the Asur king of Dinájpur, whose bloody wars with Kṛishṇa still live in the traditions of the people. From this peak, which rises on one side almost perpendicularly to a considerable height, there is a

* The Barábar Hills actually fall within the limits of the head-quarters subdivision, but their close connexion with Dharáwat renders their consideration here more appropriate. The Siddheśvara peak is believed to have been visited by the Chinese pilgrim Hiuen Tsiang, and to have been mentioned by him as a lofty mountain from the summit of which the Buddha had contemplated the kingdom of Magadha. It is hardly necessary to add that the Pali inscriptions on the famous caves show that they were excavated, four by the great Aśoka, and three (the Nágárjuní ones) by his grandson Daśaratha, for Buddhist ascetics. Later inscriptions on these caves show that they were subsequently occupied by Brahmanical ascetics. About the third or fourth century after Christ, the kings Śárdúla Varman and Ananta Varman placed Brahmanical images of Deva-mátá, of Katyáyaní, and of Mahadeva and his wife in three of the caves. At a somewhat later date, in the sixth or seventh century, the teacher Yogánanda recorded his adoration of

fine view over the country. In the month of Bhádo (September) a large fair or *melá* is held here, which is exclusively attended by men. High upon the peak of Barábar an extempore *bazár* is fitted up, and a brisk trade is driven in petty articles of all kinds, especially in sweetmeats and offerings for the god. The visitors begin to arrive with daylight, and spend the day on the hill. The night is devoted to the worship of the image, and in the morning the crowd of pilgrims begins to melt away. Judging from what I saw at my visit in 1873, the fair is not so numerously attended as in Dr. Buchanan-Hamilton's time, for he describes the plain of Rám Gaya as filled with the pilgrims; but I calculate that between 10,000 and 20,000 visitors from all parts of Bihár passed the night on the mountain. The show of *fakírs* was very curious, and as studies of the combination of dirt and sanctity they were particularly worth the attention of an artist. To the south, near the foot of this hill, the path up which is freely adorned by images of all kinds, lies a small recess enclosed on two sides by the mountain, on the third by an artificial barrier of stone, and on the fourth by a long low ridge of granite. Here in the solid rock have been cut the remarkable caves which have given the name of *Sátghar* to the glen. These four extraordinary caves in this part of the mountain average thirty-two feet by fourteen feet; and three out of the four are chiselled to a wonderful polish. The fourth is still unfinished. Inscriptions in the Pali character fix with certainty the date of the excavation of these caves. The oldest was dug in the year 252 B.C. and the latest in 214 B.C., so that they have been in existence for more than two thousand years. Not far off is the sacred spring called the *Patálgangá*; and in another spur of the hill, known as *Nágárjuní*, are the three other caves which complete the 'seven caves.' Further south, at the base of the rugged peak of Kauwádol (the 'crow's rocking-stone'), which is identified as the site of the ancient Buddhist monastery of Síla-bhadra visited by Hiuen Tsiang, is an enormous stone figure of Buddha. These antiquities have been fully described by both Dr. Buchanan-Hamilton and General Cunningham.

---

the *Siddhes'vara lingam, i.e.,* of a form of Śiva. The caves must therefore have been occupied by non-Buddhists at the time of the visit of Hiuen Tsiang in the seventh century, which accounts for his silence concerning them. At a still later date, somewhere about the twelfth century, the Yogí Karmamárga, and the pilgrim Bhayankara Nátha, visited the caves and inscribed their names. Still later the Nágárjuní caves were occupied by Musalmán fakírs. This would seem to have taken place about three or four hundred years ago. The various caves are named as follows. The four on the Barábar Hill are called respectively, the *Karan Chaupár* cave, the *Sudámá* cave, *Lomas Rikhi* cave, and the *Viswa Jhomprí* cave. The Nágárjuní caves were called in Pali, the *Gopiká Kubbhá*, the *Vapiyaká Kubbhá*, and the *Vadathiká Kubbhá*, respectively. At the present day they have no special modern names. For further particulars regarding these caves, *see* Rep. Arch. Surv. Ind. I, 40 and .

G. A. G

"Not far from these hills lies another natural curiosity. About nine miles to the north-east of the Barábar Hills, and three miles from Hulásganj, lies the village of Dapthú, which must formerly have been a place of religious celebrity, and which still contains the ruins of some handsome temples, well worth a visit. To the north of this village, again, and about two miles distant, just within the Gaya boundary, is an extraordinary monolith in the open fields. It consists of a granite column, measuring 53½ feet in length by an average of 3 feet in diameter. The capital and pedestal are quadrangular: the former is 86 inches long and 36 in diameter, while the base is 70 inches long and 40 in diameter. The shaft has 16 plain sides: at 38½ inches above the pedestal it contracts its diameter suddenly by about 3 inches. This immense column is lying horizontally on the ground, pointing north and south; about half of it is below the surface of the field. The granite of which it is composed is exactly similar to that of the Barábar Hills, and there can be no doubt that it was originally quarried there. Local tradition asserts that Rájá Sur Singh, who reigned in the Himalaya when the world was young, sent two divine messengers to bring this column from Lanká to be set up in a huge tank at Janakpur. But the gods loitered or wearied on the road, and after travelling all night, day broke on them here, and they were forced to leave their burden, to be a wonder and token to all time. Two impressions, one a each end of the pillar, mark the places where the adamantine heads of the heroes wore away the solid granite. The column possesses some sanctity. On feast-days and fast-days, and on the family festivals of the neighbouring villagers, offerings are made to the stone. Of its sacred character there can be no doubt, for it is related that Rájá Mitrajít Singh came to try and remove the column to Tikari, but the excavations made by day were filled up during the night by ghostly hands, and the awe-struck monarch, desisting from his impious attempt, bestowed the five *bighás* of land which immediately surround the stone as an endowment for a guardian Bráhman."

About four miles east of Barábar, at the village of Járú, where the river Phálgú (or Muháná) divides itself into two branches, are the ruins of an ancient mosque, dating at least from the 15th century. It stood at one end of a courtyard which was surrounded by cloisters, each cell having a small domed roof. The mosque itself is roofed by several small domes. It is built partly of brick and partly of stone, the latter being evidently taken from some older Hindu structure. Beyond the village is a chain of rugged hills, at the foot of which are occasionally seen dressed stone and other remnants of old Hindu work. On the summit of the highest peak, which is crowned by a picturesque clump of trees, is a large *lingam* known as *Hariharnáth Mahádeo.* It is said that if a pilgrim to it remains absolutely silent during his whole journey, he can encircle the *lingam* completely with his arms and hands.

AURANGABAD SUBDIVISION.

AURANGABAD (more accurately Aurangábád), the head-quarters of the subdivision, is a long straggling town on the Grand Trunk Road, about fourteen miles from the Sone river and thirty from Sherghati, in N. latitude 24° 45′ 3″ and E. longitude 84° 25′ 2″. The population of the subdivision is 472,507, of whom 226,237 are males and 246,270 females. That of the Aurangabad police jurisdiction is 258,373, of whom 121,221 are males and 137,152 females. The houses are chiefly made of mud, and some of them are adorned with carved wooden galleries. There are no remarkable temples or buildings. Besides the court-houses and jail there is a school, a dispensary, and an inspection-bungalow. The trade of the place is not important, consisting chiefly of food-grains, oil-seeds, leather, lacquered ware, glassware, and candles.

Six miles south-east of Aurangabad is Deo, an important mart and the residence of Rájá Bhíkham Náráyan Singh Bahádur, of Deo. There is an old stone sun-temple here, called the Súraj Mandir. Fairs are held here in the months of Kátik (October-November) and Chait (March-April), which are largely attended both for the purposes of traffic and to perform vows and religious obligations. One of the ceremonies consists in fastening a number of cords to a hook in the roof of the temple, which are extended to represent the rays of the sun. To the south-east of the town there is a tank sacred to the sun, and close by another, celebrated for its lotuses. Six miles east of Deo is the little village of Umgá, close to which, on a hill, there is a ruined temple sacred to Mahádeva, very similar to the one at Deo. A large fair is held here on the full moon of Pús (December-January). This place was formely the head-quarters of the Deo family, and the two villages are commonly spoken of together in one word as Deomungá.

The present Rájá of Deo traces his descent from Mahárání Rái Bhán Singh, a younger brother of the Ráná of Udaipur, one of the Sisaudiá Rájputs. This prince, on his way to the shrine of Jagannáth, encamped at Umgá. There was a hill-fort here, the chief of which had recently died, leaving an old and helpless widow, who was unable to keep order over her mutinous subjects. On hearing of Bhán Singh's arrival, she put herself under his protection, adopting him as her son. He soon made himself master of the Umgá fort, and quelled the incipient rebellion. After his death two of his descendants ruled here, but the fort was subsequently deserted in favour of the present seat of the family of Deo. Rájá Chhatarpati, from whom the present Rájá is sixth in descent, was the first to espouse the cause of the English. In the contest between Warren Hastings and Chet Singh, the Rájá of Banáras, the Deo Rájá being too old to take the field in person, sent his son, Fat'h Náráyan Singh, to join the English forces under Major

Crawford. He afterwards aided the English under Major Russell in the war with the Pindárís. For the former service the young Rájá was given a *nánkár*, or rent-free tenure, of eleven villages. His subsequent services were rewarded with the Ráj of Palámau, which was afterwards exchanged for certain villages in the district of Gaya, yielding a profit of Rs. 3,000 per annum. The successor of Fat'h Náráyan Singh was Ghanshám Singh. He also took the field with the British forces against the mutineers in Sargújá, and received in recompense, a second time, the Ráj of Palámau. His son, Rájá Mitra Bhán Singh, rendered good service in quelling the Kol insurrection in Chotá (Chutiá) Nágpur, and was rewarded with the remission of Rs. 1,000 from the Government revenue accruing from the Deo estate. The services of the present Rájá's father, Jai Prákash Singh, during the Mutiny of 1857, and the aid he afforded to Colonel Dalton in quelling the insurrection in Chotá Nágpur, were recognised with the titles of Maharajah Bahádur and the Order of the Star of India. He was also granted a *jágír*, or rent-free tenure, in *parganas* Roh and Samai and the village Bámhan Ḍíh in *pargana* Sherghati, yielding an annual revenue of over Rs. 10,000.

About three miles south-west of Aurangabad, on the right bank of the river Batáná, is the ancient village of Pawaí, with a fort, a temple, and a tank. It was once the seat of a Rájá, but the family has lost its former importance. Six miles to the north-west, on the east of the river Punpun, the large village of Jamhor, principally inhabited by Agarwálás, marks the confluence of the Batáná and Punpun rivers, and a fair is accordingly held there on the full moon of Kátik (October-November). About four miles north-east of Jamhor lies Obrá, a centre of carpet-manufacture, at the confluence of the Adrí and the Punpun. It contains a police-outpost, with a force of 1 head-constable and 4 constables. The richest inhabitants of the town are Súñrís by caste, but the carpet-makers are Musalmáns. Two miles to the north-west of Obrá the village of Kárá is remarkable as the residence of one of the principal Muhammadan families of the district. About three miles south-west of Jamhor, on the bank of the Punpun, is the village of Siris, inhabited by large numbers of Káyasth families, whose members are widely scattered over Bihár in Government service. An old mosque here was built by the Emperor Aurangzeb, who rested at Siris, when marching through Bihár. Chirkáñwáñ, with the adjoining village of Rafiganj, nearly the largest village of the subdivision, is the seat of a large cattle-fair held during the festival of the Bisuá, and also has a considerable trade in blankets. Rafiganj contains an independent police-outpost, with a force of 1 sub-inspector and 4 constables. Within five miles of Rafiganj to the south and south-east are the villages of Cheoñ and Deokulí. In the first are some old temples, and, on a hill named Pachhár, a south-facing cave, with a figure of

Máyá Deví inside. In the hills falling within the boundaries of the second village are numerous small caves. At Deokulí, on the river Dháwá, there are remains of statues, &c. Between Rafíganj and Madanpur lie the Mándá hills, in which are several remains, consisting of statues and the like.

Other important marts in Aurangabad police jurisdiction are Bharúb, Khudwá, Kasimá, Madanpur (with a police-outpost, 1 head-constable and 4 constables), Khiriyáwáñ, Wár (with an ancient fort), and Pogar.

The only other place that need be noted is Bárun, with a police-outpost (1 head-constable and 4 constables), on the Sone, situated in N. latitude 24° 51′ 35″ and E. longitude 84° 15′ 57″. The river at this point is crossed by the Grand Trunk Road. During the rains the causeway, on which the road is made, lies under water, and travellers must use the ferry. About half a mile south of the causeway has been constructed an *anicut* or weir, to divert the waters of the Sone into the Eastern and Western Main Canals. An account of this weir and the works in connection with it will be found in the statistical account of Shahabad district.

NABINAGAR (more accurately Nabínagar), 18 miles south of Aurangabad, a police-station, is situated on the left bank of the Punpun. The police force consists of 1 sub-inspector, 1 head-constable, and 9 constables. The population of the jurisdiction is 108,033, of whom 52,135 are males and 55,898 females. Near by is Chandragaṛh, the fort of the moon, the residence of a family of Chauhán Rájpúts, coming originally from Mewár. The fort was built in 1102 *Faslí*, or 1694 A.D. The ancestors of the present family were two cousins, Ugra Náráyan Singh and Partáp Náráyan Singh, each of whom owned eight annas of the property. Ugra Náráyan's son was Ráy Hit Náráyan Singh Bahádur, whose grandson is Babu Naurang Deo Náráyan Singh and the present owner of eight annas of the property. The share of Partáp Náráyan Singh is much divided. His great-grandson, the owner of two annas, is a minor under the Court of Wards. One of Partáp's sons was Ráy Mahíp Náráyan Singh Bahádur, and a grandson by another son was Ráy Lachhmí Náráyan Singh Bahádur. These three Ráy Bahádurs got their titles and a sword and a lákhiraj grant of Rs. 1,000 each, for good services done in the Mutiny. In the town of Nabinagar there is a tiled hut, known as the temple of Sokhá Bábá, where persons suffering from snake-bite are brought as a last resource. If the person bitten recovers, clarified butter and molasses are offered to Sokhá Bábá. Nabinagar carries on a large trade in blankets and brass vessels. It has a special reputation for these latter articles.

Four miles south of Nabinagar, on the right bank of the Punpun, the market of Ṭañrwá is the emporium for articles coming from the south, and is inhabited by numerous families of turners (*kharádi*), who make wooden cups, boxes, toys, etc.

About seven miles east of Nabinagar is the ancient village of Kuṭumbá with a police-outpost and a force of 1 head-constable and 4 constables. It is principally inhabited by Musalmáns, and is falling into decay. The village gives its name to a *pargana* which is now principally owned by some Bengáli *zamindars*. South of the village are the ruins of a large moated fort. Four miles south-east the important mart of Mahárájganj lies on the borders of the Palámau and Gaya jurisdictions.

Máli was once the seat of an important noble family, which is now reduced to poverty.

Other important villages of the Nabinagar jurisdiction are Kenduá, Barem, Kaker, and Mahuáwáñ.

Daudnagar (more accurately Dáúdnagar), on the Sone Canal and near the right bank of the river Sone, is situated about the middle of the western frontier of the district. It is a town of some importance, with municipal institutions, a hospital and a police-station (a force of 1 sub-inspector, 1 head-constable, and 9 constables), and was founded by Dáúd Khán, a *risáldár* of Aurangzeb, who gave him the parganas of Anchhá, Manorá, and Goh as a reward for conquering Palámau. Members of his family still reside here, in receipt of a pension. The population of the police jurisdiction is 106,101, of whom 52,881 are males and 53,220 females. The town is conveniently placed on the main route from Benares to Gaya, and at first prospered exceedingly. It is surrounded by a moat, and till a few years ago had gates, which were regularly shut every night. A short way out of the town is Ahmadganj, which was founded by Ahmad Khán, grandson of Dáúd Khán, and contains his tomb. Its trade was once very considerable, but the opening of the Sone Canal, with its through steamer traffic, is ruining it. It has still some trade in brass vessels, blankets, carpets, sesamum, linseed, and molasses, and it is hoped that its importance will revive when a dock which has been lately built for the use of canal boats has come more into use. In Dr. Buchanan-Hamilton's time there was a cloth-factory dependent on the commercial resident at Patna, and factory of the Opium Agent at that city. The latter still exists. The cloth-factory has been abolished, but the manufacture of cloth is continued. Coarse carpets and blankets are also manufactured. The ruined mosque and serai to the west of the town contain fine examples of Musálman architecture.

Eight miles north of Daudnagar, on the right bank of the canal, Shamshernagar, founded by Shamsher Khán, a descendant of Dáúd Khán, is an important village with a ruined fort and a beautiful mosque.

The latter has lately been repaired under the superintendence of the Archæological Survey.

Fourteen miles to the east, on the main road to Gaya, the important village of Goh contains a police-outpost (with a force of 1 sub-inspector and 4 constables), and is principally inhabited by Rájputs and Bráhmans. Cultivation is somewhat neglected in consequence. Between Goh and Daudnagar are the villages of Dehorá, on the bank of the Punpun, and Sihárí, the latter of which has many wells and groves and a beautifully carved miniature stone temple.

Other important towns in the jurisdiction of Daudnagar are Malhad, Koiláwáñ, Hamídnagar, Dádar, and Gopálpur. Deokuṇḍ, which falls within the geographical limits of this police-station, has been more conveniently dealt with in describing the Arwal jurisdiction of the Jahanabad subdivision.

I close this sketch of the towns and villages of Gaya district with an account of the travels of Hiuen Tsiang, the famous Chinese pilgrim, who visited India in the seventh century of our era. At that time this district formed part of the great kingdom of Magadha, which extended south of the Ganges from Banáras to Monghyr and southwards as far as Bodh Gayá. The pilgrim had been in Nepál, and entered Magadha about the 20th February 637 A.D. After visiting Patna he marched south thirty-three miles to Ti-lo-shi-kia or Tiláḍaka, which was almost on the site of the village Tiláṛá, on the east bank of the Phálgú; thence south again to Buddha's Mountain, probably the main peak of the Barábar Hills. Thence, after visiting the large monastery of Gunamatí, at Dharáwat, and Sílabhadra, another monastery on an isolated hill, probably the hill of Kauwáḍol, he went south-west to Gaya. He found that place thinly peopled, but containing a thousand families of Bráhmans. On his way to Bodh Gayá he made a detour to Po-lo-ki-pu-ti or Prágbodhi, a hill on the east bank of the Phálgú. After paying his respects to the Tree of Wisdom, the pilgrim crossed the river again to Bakraur, where there was the *stupa,* already mentioned, set up in honour of Gandhahasti, or the scented elephant, and also a tank and a stone pillar, the ruins of which still exist. The pilgrim then marched north-east in the direction of Rájgir (Rájagṛiha). His way led him by Kuṛkihár (Kukkuṭa-páda-giri), Tapoban, Jeṭhian (Yashṭivana), and Budhain (Buddhavana), which he duly visited and described. The rest of his journey was nearly all in Patna district, and need not be dwelt upon here.

CHAPTER III.

The systems of Land Measurement.

The standard of measurement is the *laggí*, the length of which varies throughout the district. The two most common ones are the "Lál darwázá" *laggí*, that adopted in the Tikari estate, and the opium *laggí*, or that used by the Opium Department.

One square *laggí* is called a *dhur*, 20 *dhurs* make one cottah (*katthá*), and 20 cottahs make one *bigha*.

The Bengal standard *laggí* of six feet and *bigha* of 1,600 square yards are not in use in the district.

The following shows the lengths of the different *laggís* above referred to:—

The standard *laggí* is 6 feet; the Lál darwázá *laggí* is 6 cubits, or 9 feet;* the opium *laggí* is $5\frac{1}{2}$ cubits, or $8\frac{1}{4}$ feet.

The standard *bigha* of 1,600 square yards is very nearly one-third of an acre of 4,840 square yards.

Four Lál darwázá *bighas* equal 9 standard *bighas*, and therefore equal about 3 acres. Therefore one Lál darwázá *bigha* $= \frac{3}{4}$ of an acre.

Sixteen opium *bighas* equal exactly ten acres. Therefore one opium *bigha* $= \frac{5}{8}$ of an acre. Therefore an acre $=$ 3 standard *bighas* $= 1\frac{1}{3}$ Lál darwázá $= 1\frac{3}{5}$ opium *bighas*.

One standard *bigha* $= \frac{1}{3}$ of an acre $= \frac{4}{9}$ of a Lál darwázá *bigha* $= \frac{8}{15}$ of an opium *bigha*.

One Lál darwázá *bigha* $= \frac{3}{4}$ of an acre $= 2\frac{1}{4}$ standard *bighas* $= 1\frac{1}{5}$ opium *bighas*.

One opium *bigha* $= \frac{5}{8}$ of an acre $= 1\frac{7}{8}$ standard *bighas* $= \frac{5}{6}$ of a Lál darwázá *bigha*.

The local seer varies in every bazár, and the one adopted in these notes weighs about 52 Company's *tolás*. It is therefore $\frac{13}{20}$ of a standard seer, and the local maund is $\frac{13}{20}$ of a standard maund. In calculating outturns, it can easily be shown that the number of local maunds per opium *bigha*, which is the local *bigha* adopted throughout these notes, unless otherwise stated, is very nearly the same as the number of standard maunds per acre.

Let A be the number of local maunds per opium *bigha*.

Then one opium bigha $= \frac{5}{8}$ of an acre; therefore there are $\frac{8}{5}$A local maunds per acre.

But one local maund $= \frac{13}{20}$ of a standard maund.

$\therefore$ there are $\frac{8}{5} A \times \frac{13}{20}$ standard maunds per acre.

$$\frac{8}{5} A \times \frac{13}{20} = A\left(1 + \frac{1}{25}\right)$$

---

* It is really more accurately about 8 feet 11 inches, but 9 feet is quite near enough for all practical purposes.

Therefore A local maunds per local bigha are equivalent to $A \times \frac{A}{25}$ standard maunds per acre, and as $\frac{A}{25}$ is very small, it may be neglected in dealing with round numbers.

Therefore, in dealing with round numbers, A local maunds per local bigha are equivalent to the same number of standard maunds per acre.

This is a very convenient fact to remember.

CHAPTER IV.

System of Irrigation.

THE district of Gaya is distinguished from every other district in the province, except Patna and Monghyr, by a conjunction of two peculiarities—a stiff clay soil and a strong slope from south to north.

This conjunction affects the whole system of agriculture and land tenures, and hence it will be found that in both of these particulars the district differs from any other in which its administrators may have gained experience. Whether that experience has been gained in the north Gangetic districts of Bihár, or in Lower Bengal, all preconceived ideas must be abandoned when approaching the thorny question of Gaya land tenures. Systems condemned elsewhere will be found to be the only possible ones here, and systems which in other districts have resulted in success will be found in Gaya to lead to disastrous consequences.

The present chapter will deal with the irrigation, upon which the whole agricultural system of the district depends. It must be understood, however, that the following remarks apply only to about four-fifths of the district, that portion to the east of the river Punpun. West of that river the Sone canals have revolutionised the relations of landlord and tenant, and the conditions of the country closely accord with those which we find prevailing in the neighbouring canal irrigated district of Shahabad.

Taking, therefore, the country to the east of the Punpun, two things at once strike us in its physical configuration.

The first is the strong slope of the country from south to north. This slope averages about 4 feet to the mile.

The other is that the district is divided, so to speak, into a number of parallel strips separated by some eight wide rivers,* which run in approximately parallel directions from south to north.

* Say, the Punpun, Morhar, Phálgú, Ḍháḍhar, Tilaiyá, Dhanárjay, Khurí, and Sakrí, but these rivers are so frequently subdivided each into two or more streams, that the enumeration must not be taken as accurate.

Each of these parallel strips is higher in the centre, and slopes down on each side to the rivers forming its eastern and western boundaries; so that a section of the district from east to west would represent a series of undulations each separated by a river. Thus,—

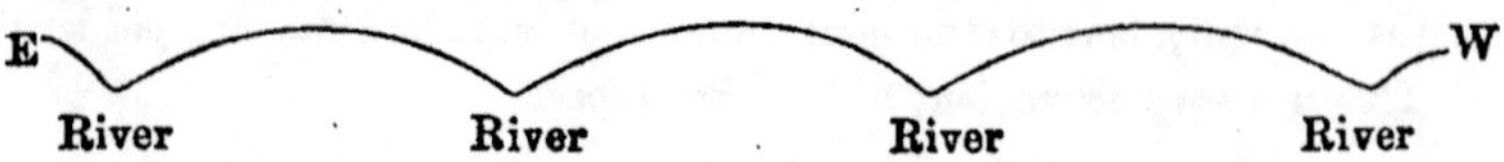

These rivers have wide* sandy beds, and are nearly dry during the greater portion of the year. In flood time they are full, and are frequently deep and dangerous torrents, but, owing to the rapid slope of the district from south to north, the water is very quickly carried off, and these floods rarely last for more than a few days.

The strips of land between the rivers may be considered as mainly rice-growing ones. The soil is a stiff clay, in some places black cotton soil, and in others red, but everywhere of the same stiff unyielding nature.

The central higher portions of these strips, known as *ṭáñṛ* lands, can rarely be irrigated, and are not fitted for rice cultivation. They are reserved for rabi (spring) and bhadoí (autumn) crops. The water level is very low, and wells are scarce and difficult to excavate. Hence these crops depend entirely on surface moisture fed by rain water. They are in consequence called *apṭá*, unirrigated.

On the slopes leading down to the rivers on each side, and in hollows in the higher ground, irrigation is possible, and here we have the richer rice lands.

In these lower lands wells are extensively used for sugarcane and rabi cultivation, and nearer the villages for poppy. These crops being cultivated with well water are called *paṭáol*, irrigated.

We therefore have, for present purposes, three kinds of crops to deal with:—

(1) The lower rabi land irrigated with well water. This will form the subject of subsequent discussion;

(2) The rice lands irrrigated in the manner subsequently to be described; and

(3) The high *ṭáñṛ* in which bhadoi and rabi crops are grown without irrigation.

	Feet.
* Width of the Phálgú	2,795
" " Ḍháḍhar	1,050
" " Tilaiyá	425
" " Dhanárjay	384
" " Khurí	940

The above are the widths of these rivers, bank to bank, where they are crossed by the Gaya-Nawádah road.

These last will be considered first. The facts to be faced by the agriculturalist are (1) a strong slope of the country from south to north, (2) a stiff clayey soil, (3) well irrigation difficult or impossible, and (4) the fact that moisture in the ground is necessary for the successful maturing of the crops.

This moisture is usually provided directly by rainfall, which, falling on the ground, becomes surface water. The soil being naturally stiff refuses to absorb it, and, were it not for artificial appliances, the water would at once flow off, down to the north and ultimately into the Ganges, leaving the soil as devoid of moisture as before. This surface water is known as *ṭháṭhe*, or *ṭhaṭṭhe, ká páni*.

To prevent this, a series of low retaining banks are built across the line of drainage of the country. These are connected by other banks running north and south, enclosing spaces of, say, forty to fifty acres. These spaces are again subdivided by lower banks running both ways, so that the whole series resembles an enormous chessboard. The main banks may be four feet high, and the subordinate ones half that in elevation. The inner squares may average an acre in size each. The outer main embankment, encircling the whole, is called *gherawá*, the inner banks are called *geñṛá* or *khaṇḍaut*, and the ultimate inner fields are called *kiárí*.

It will be seen that this series of banks is admirably adapted for retaining the surface water. Not a drop of rain water is allowed to flow beyond the limits of the particular *kiárí* in which it falls, and the stiff soil is given ample time to absorb the moisture.

With such a strong slope in the country it may be imagined that these earthworks are subjected to great wear and tear, and have to be constantly mended and put in good order. Even one excessive rainfall will often sweep them entirely away over large areas. They are thus a constant source of expense to the landlord who keeps them in order, and the earthwork involved gives valuable employment to large numbers of people at the time when it is most needed, viz., the hot weather after the spring crops are cut.

Earthwork in Gaya is called *gilandází*, or earth-throwing, and the special kind of earthwork above described is known as *geñṛábandí*, It is rightly said that *gilandází* is the life of Gaya. Unfortunately mistaken motives of economy have led some landlords, who should know better, to content themselves with the mere enunciation of the proposition without carrying it into practice. There is no more profitable speculation than *geñṛábandí*. The writer has known instances where expenditure on it gave at once a profit of 43 per cent. per annum on the capital, and he has never known it give less than 30 per cent. It converts absolutely barren soil into fertile fields.

We shall now take the second class of lands—the irrigated rice lands—grown on the lower ground which is capable of irrigation.

Here we have the following facts to consider: a soil and a slope the same as in the last case, and the fact that surface moisture is not sufficient for the crop.

The importance of a complete solution of this problem may be gauged from the fact that some 50 per cent. of the whole cultivated area of the district is under rice.* Officers whose experience has been acquired in the north Gangetic districts of Bihár, or who have been brought up in the belief that Bihár is not a rice-eating country, will find it difficult to understand that what is true of the rest of Bihár is not true of Gaya. In Gaya, all classes above the lowest labouring classes eat rice with more or less regularity. Rice is the main food stock of the district. The country of Magadha, of which Gaya forms a large portion, has been famous for its rice for at least thirteen hundred years. The "Patna rice" of our childhood's days, takes its name from the chief emporium of Magadha; and the Chinese pilgrim Hiuen Tsiang, who visited India about the year 600 A.D., not only praises the delicious flavour of the Gaya rice, but tells a legend of a heretic king who was converted to Buddhism through the means of its fragrant scent.

Rice requires water in large quantities for its successful cultivation. It specially requires water at two seasons—in the month of *Asáṛh* (June—July) for transplanting, and in the lunar asterism of *Hathiyá* (end of September or beginning of October), when it is wanted for giving body to the grain which is being formed. At the former of these two seasons the fields have not only to be wet, they have to be flooded with water. At the latter, water is wanted within a critical period of a few days, during which there is frequently no rain.

Rice land is irrigated in two ways. If it is on sloping ground, at the foot of high ground, it can be irrigated on the *geñṛábandí* system, the surface water of the higher ground being collected, stored up, and used as wanted. Land adapted for such irrigation is, however, of limited extent, and far the greater portion of the rice of the district is supplied with water by means of what is called the "*pain* and *áhar* system."

This system is peculiar to Gaya, and deserves careful study. It is first necessary to understand what an *áhar* is. An *áhar* is a reservoir for water, formed by embanking on three sides a piece of high ground. It is usually on the highest land in a village, and the open side is still higher ground, so that if the whole were full of water, none would run out unless the bank were cut. If no higher ground is available, then

---

* It must not be forgotten that besides this a large quantity of rabi land, about 20 per cent. of the whole cultivated area of the district, is also irrigated by *gilandázi*, and hence pays rent in kind. This makes up the 70 per cent. mentioned on page 69.

the *áhar* is embanked on all four sides. It must be clearly understood that an *áhar* is in no way dug like a tank. It is built *on* the surface of the ground, and, from its position, its bottom is higher than the other land of the village which it is intended to irrigate. When irrigation is wanted, all that has to be done is to cut the embankment, when the water will descend by gravitation.

The following rough sketch will give an idea of the shape of an *áhar*:—

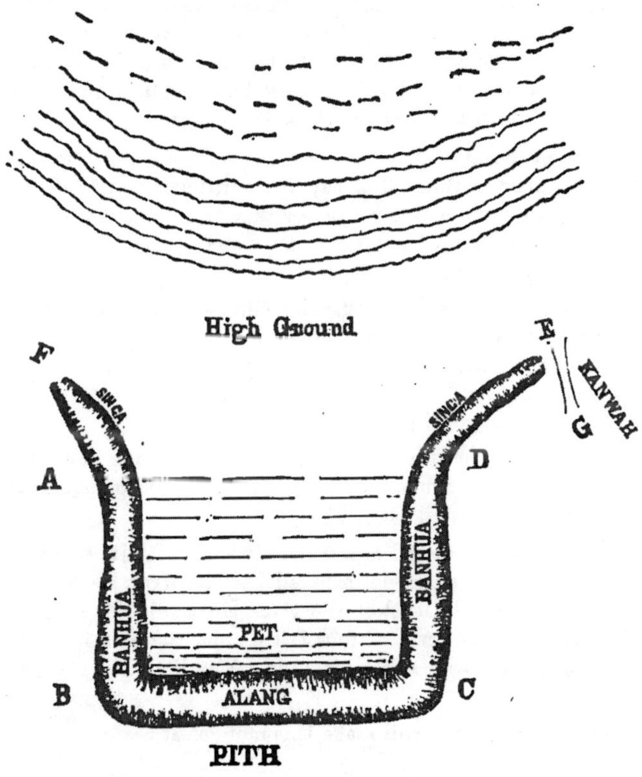

Here AB and CD are the two side banks of the *áhar*, going as it were down the slope of a hill. The slope is, of course, very slight. It is often hardly visible to the eye. BC is the strong embankment at the foot. These banks are called *piṇḍ*, but the main bank BC is specially called the *alang*. Sometimes training banks AF and DE are added, to conduct surface water into the *áhar*.

The bed of the *áhar*, inside the embankment, is called the *péṭ* or belly, and the portion behind and below the *alang* or main embankment is called the *píṭh* or back. The two side banks are called the *bañhuá* or arms, and the training banks AF and DE are called the *singá* or horns. The *áhar* is only intended to hold water within the square ABCD, being deep near BC, and getting shallower and shallower up to AD. To prevent an overflow, a drain EG, called a *kanwah*, is usually provided. It is simply a ditch.

In order to use the water, a masonry spill-dam (*chhilká* or *chahká*) is provided in one of the three sides. This is not quite so high as the embankment, so that it acts as a safety-sluice, and carries the water away before it can top the former. It has masonry parapets to prevent the spill-water washing away the embankment at the sides. These are called *janghá* or thighs. An arched tunnel with a sluice gate through the bottom of the *chhilká* allows the water to be drawn off as required. This arched tunnel is called the *bhauñh* or eyebrow.

Áhars may be all sizes. In some the sides are even two miles long. An average *áhar*, with a *péṭ* of say a hundred acres, costs about Rs. 325 to make, at the rate of one rupee per thousand cubic feet of earthwork, which is that paid by landlords. An *aharí* is a small *áhar*, and may be only an acre in area.

The water from the *áhar* is usually allowed to flow from field to field as required, in rotation. This method of irrigation is called *chhánan* or *melwán*. When the water has to be raised, by throwing it up to a field of a higher level from a lower one (*e.g.*, with baskets), the method of irrigation is called *chhích*.

An *áhar*, it will be seen, is well adapted for catching and retaining the surface water. But this is rarely sufficient. It has generally also to be fed by a *pain*.

A *pain* may be described as a water channel, with its source of supply in a river bed, and carried down parallel to the river, its course being so selected that while the level of the river sinks with the general slope of the country at the rate of four feet a mile, the *pain* is kept as much as possible at the level of the spot at which it takes in its supply of water.

The following sketch will make this more clear :—

North

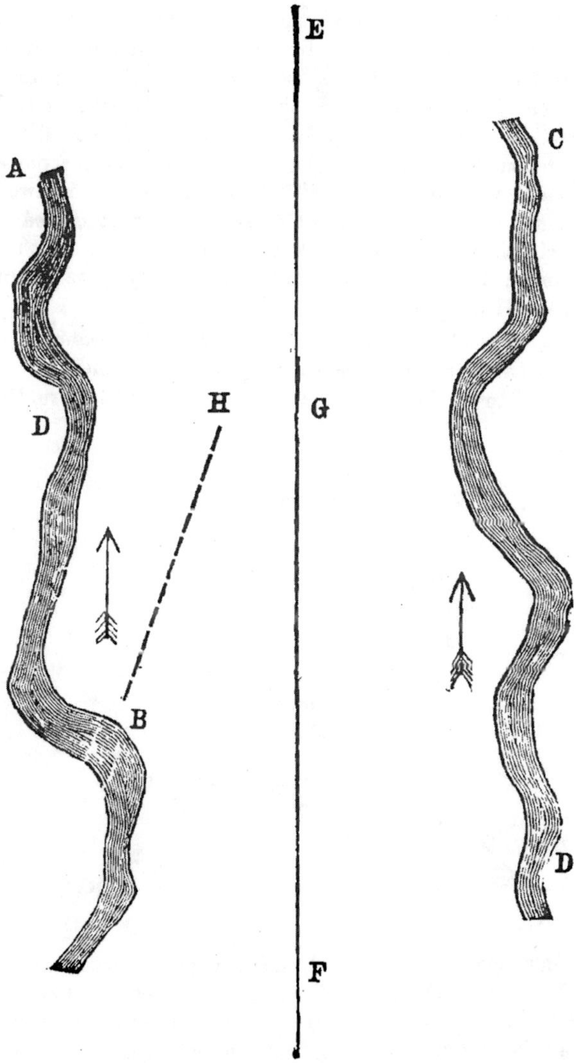

South

AB and CD are two rivers running from south to north, on a slope of four feet to the mile. Assume that the distance from B to D is two miles in a direct line, and then it follows that D is eight feet lower than B. But the ground between the two rivers rises from each, and the highest line or water-shed, so to speak, of the undulation will be along the line EF. Assume that the rise of the country is, say, ten feet from the river AB to the line EF. Then the point G, opposite D, on the line EF, will be ten feet higher than D; and somewhere between D and G, say at H, the land will be seven feet higher than D, that is to say, one foot lower than B. If we take a water channel, commencing at B, and following the course of the dotted line to H, the water will run along it with a fall of one foot in two miles, or of six inches to the mile. If we make an *áhar* at H, fed by the channel BH, then it will hold a store of water, from which all the country between H and D can be easily irrigated by mere gravitation. This channel BH is a *pain*.

One thing has to be noted. In order to catch the water of a river, the mouth of the *pain* must face the deep current of the river as much as possible, and to do this advantage must be taken of a curve, thus—

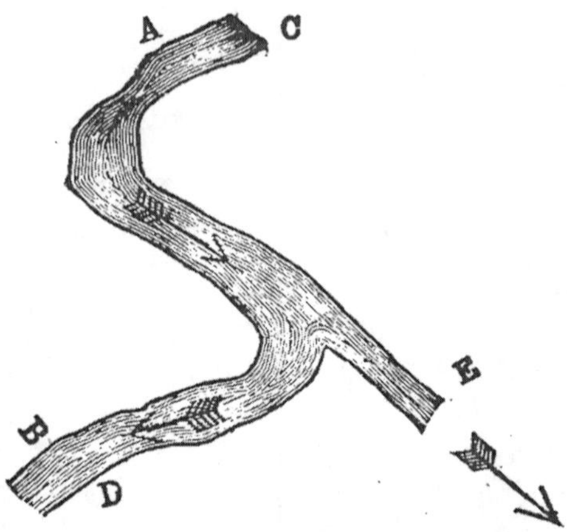

ABCD is a curve in a river bed, CD being the outer bank. Then the *pain* EF must take off at E in the outer bank. But the outer bank of a curve in a river is always a high one, and the ground level there is, in this district, usually eight or ten feet higher than the bed of the river, so that the *pain* starts at first a good way below the level of the country. It hence follows that, unless the slope of the country is very rapid, a *pain* can rarely fill an *áhar* near its head where it takes off from the river. It is usually two or three miles before the water of a *pain* reaches the level of the cultivation, and can flow into the *áhars*, and give them a supply of water sufficient for irrigation. A *pain* is, however, often as much as ten or twelve miles in length (the writer has seen one twenty miles long), and serves many villages, each with several *áhars* covering a large area of country. The owner of each village served has his regularly agreed upon turn (or *pάrá*) for the use of the *pain*, and contributes a proportionate quota towards the cost of keeping it up.

A *pain* serves automatically during the river floods in the rainy season, after the close of which, when the supply of water in the river falls short, training works are made in the bed of the river, or the whole bed is embanked across, and the water raised to the level of the mouth of the *pain*. These *pains* sometimes taking off at as short a distance as half a mile from each other, it follows that when the river is embanked opposite any one, those below are dependent entirely upon the percolation of the sandy river bed, and derive a proportionately small supply as their reach of river bed is short.

Pains silt up very rapidly with sand and deposit, and have to be constantly deepened. So also the training works in the river beds have to be undertaken again and again as often as the river falls below the level of the mouth of the *pain*, and are washed away again with each rise. Nevertheless, the benefits derived from these training works are so great that, in a single year, *pain* owners persist in making them over and over again as they are washed away.

If the rivers had a constant supply of water, the *pains* alone would be sufficient, but, owing to the slope of the country, the former are nothing but wide mountain torrents, and are nearly dry for the greater portion of the year. A flood may come down for a week or two in the rains, and then the beds again become nearly dry, and there are rarely more than three or four of such floods during one rainy season.

Hence the *pains* alone are not sufficient for irrigation. They only carry water when the rivers are full, and that may be a time, and usually is a time, when the rainfall is plenteous and sufficient for the rice. Their main use, therefore, is to fill the *áhars*, in which water is stored up for critical periods, especially for the rice transplantation and for the *hathiyá* asterism. These *áhars* are store-houses, or, as the natives expressively name them, *khazánás* (treasuries) of water. They provide the water for the irrigation of the drier kinds of rice sown in the lands immediately below them, and also allow the damper rices to be sown in their own beds. When the rice crop is cut, and all the water run off, the damp beds are again largely used for unirrigated spring crops, especially wheat. In this situation only can sufficient moisture be depended upon, unless well irrigation be possible.

It should be noted that, when possible, *pains* are also freely used for direct irrigation, without the intervention of *áhars*, and this is most often the case in the cold season, when they are supplied constantly with a moderate amount of water by training works. This water is very useful for the spring crops, but it must always be borne in mind that the main use of a *pain* is to fill the *áhars* connected with it.

Channels of water are divided into two classes—*kudartí*, natural, and *masnuí*, artificial. A *pain* falls under the latter head. A large *pain* which serves several villages is called a *dasiain pain*. *Pains* have often sub-channels or branches, which are to the parent *pain* what the *pain* is to the river. Such a branch is called a *bhoklá*. The mouth or intake of a *pain* or *bhoklá* is called the *mohánâ* or *muñh*. When the level of a river is raised by a cross embankment, so as to give water to a *pain*, the embankment is called a *báñdh*. A similar embankment across a *pain*, so as to give water to a *bhoklá*, is called a *garáñṛí*. These latter are made by first tying fascines (called *gúñṛ* or *morá*) of straw or branches to a line of posts (*khúñṭá*) planted across the *pain*. This is used as a foundation, on which is thrown earth (*miṭṭí*) and sods (*chípá*).

The training works consist of a large hollow made in the sandy bed of a river, into which the water in the surrounding portion of the bed percolates and collects. This hollow is called a *ḍabúr* or *ahór*. From this a channel, called *naréh*, leads to the mouth of the *pain*.

The end of a *pain* or *bhoklá* from which the water issues into an *áhar*, is called the *baharain*.

It will thus be seen that the system of *pain* and *áhar* irrigation is a peculiar one, and admirably adapted to the necessities of the country. A district which, but for this system, would be almost entirely a dry and barren plain, is covered with cultivated fields of rice. It is a system which not only makes cultivation possible, but which, when in full working order, is an insurance against famine. Indeed the writer believes that, under present circumstances, a general scarcity in Gaya district is, humanly speaking, an impossibility. Crops may fail, and do fail, in villages or tracts not served or imperfectly served by *pains*, but fortunately the area of such tracts is not great.

But all this *gilandází*, as it is called, must be kept strong and in good order. A sharp lesson was shown by the partial scarcity of 1888-89.

For several years the seasons had been generally unfavourable. The landlords had become impoverished, and had neglected to keep the embankments which form the backbone of the *gilandází* system in good order. In 1888 there came sudden and violent floods, which the weakened banks could not withstand, and they were swept away over wide areas. Hence the rice crop of 1888-89 was in parts of the district a total failure.

The lesson was not lost upon Government, and loans under the Land Improvement Act were freely issued to landholders in those parts of the district (especially the Nawádah subdivision) in which the embankments were broken down. They were put into thorough repair, and in the year 1891-92, the Nawádah subdivision gave excellent rice, while in the south of the district, where there are no *pains*, the crops have been a total failure.

The cost of making *pains* varies, of course, with their size and length, but an idea may be gained from the fact that an average *pain* may generally be put down as representing a capital expenditure of a thousand rupees a mile.

It is impossible to calculate the capital expenditure invested in this kind of insurance over the whole district, but the writer does not hesitate to say that it must amount to crores of rupees.

The final question to be answered is, who found all this capital? Who designs and pays for these elaborate and successful systems of irrigation? Single *raiyats* cannot find the capital. Groups of *raiyats* cannot combine together to dig a channel perhaps ten miles long, and serving many villages. The only capitalists available are the landlords. The landlords alone can dig and clear the *pains*, and throw up embankments and keep them in order. To them, accordingly, falls the duty and expense of maintaining the *gilandází*, and it may be stated that a landlord is considered to do his duty when he spends one-ninth of the rent he realizes for this purpose.

But the *raiyat* must be secured: without *gilandází* he would get no crops, and, as human nature is human nature all the world over, if he paid a fixed cash rent to his landlord, the latter would be likely to neglect his duties and to let the tenant be ruined. By mutual agreement, therefore, the relation of landlord and tenant is fixed on a basis which makes the amount of the landlord's rent depend entirely on the amount of *gilandází* which he does. The consideration of this relationship of landlord and tenant in Gaya will be considered in the following chapter.

The irrigation of the lower rabi lands with well water presents no features which are not met in other Bihár districts.

Well water is raised either by bullocks, with the *moṭ*, or by hand with the well-lever or *láṭhá*. The former is rarely met with in the agriculture of Gaya, but the long swaying *láṭhá* is a prominent feature in the landscape everywhere. Rude wells are dug in the fields, when the water is near the surface and can be raised by the lever. These wells are called *kúáñ*, as distinct from the *inárá* or masonry well. According to the supply of water, one, two, three or even more levers work simultaneously at a single *kúáñ*. The sides of a *kúáñ* are built up with earthen rings called *gaṛuá*, and sometimes, in sandy soils, where wood is cheap, with wooden rings called *ḍól*. For other particulars regarding wells and well-levers the reader is referred to *Bihar Peasant Life*, in which minute detailed descriptions of both will be found.

The main spring crops irrigated with well water are poppy, wheat and sugarcane. Of these poppy is the principal.

In November 1891, a series of experiments in poppy irrigation were made in Gaya district, and it was found that under ordinary circumstances a well-lever with a well of average depth, irrigated about ten cottahs of poppy a day, and, allowing for watering the same plot over again at the proper intervals, commanded two acres of ground, which it covered with about one and-a-half inches of water every twelve days. Full particulars of these experiments are given in Appendix A to this chapter. In another appendix (B) are given the principal native words used in connection with irrigation in this district.

APPENDIX A.

Note on well-lever (láṭhá) irrigation in Gaya District, founded on a series of experiments conducted by Mr. Grierson in various parts of Pargana Goh, and by Mr. Lang at Head-quarters.

The amount of water raised in a day depends on the depth of the well. The depths of wells in Bihár are measured by *porsás*. One *porsá* may be taken as representing seven feet.

The contents of a well bucket may be taken as two gallons. All those measured by Mr. Lang contained just that amount, except one which measured 2¼ gallons. Those measured by Mr. Grierson contained each, when raised to the surface, just 12 reputed quart bottles = 2 gallons, except in one instance which gave 13 bottles or 2⅙ gallons.

The standard bigha contains 1,600 sq. yards, say ⅓ of an acre of 4,840 sq. yards. The local bigha varies in Gaya district. Wherever the experiments were made, the local bigha was measured with the "Lál Darwázá" *laggí*. 20 L. D. *laggís* = 30 standard *laggís*. Twenty sq. *laggís* make one bigha.

∴ one L. D. bigha = 30^2 standard sq. *laggís* = 900 standard sq. *laggís* = 2¼ standard bighas.

∴ 4 L. D. bighas = 9 standard bighas = say, 3 acres.

A well lever is worked by two men, taking turns. The man off duty at the lever busies himself in the field, conducting the water. Near Gaya the average day's work is 10 hours. In the *mufassal*, men work for twelve hours.

The following are selections from the various experiments :—

The area covered three inches deep by one month's work is first calculated from the contents of the well bucket and the number of times it is raised in a day; and then the result is checked by the area which a well lever is found by actual experiment to command. All these figures refer to the month of November, when water is still not very far from the surface.

CASE No. 1.

Average of a number of cases in Pargana Goh.

Depth of well, $2\frac{1}{2}$ to 3 *porsás,* say 20 ft.
Contents of bucket, 2 gals.
Number of times raised in $\frac{1}{2}$ an hour; 120 to 130, say 125.
Working day=12 hours.

∴ the amount of water raised per diem

$= 2 \times 125 \times 2 \times 12 = 6{,}000$ gals.

$= 60{,}000$ lbs. $= \frac{60{,}000}{62{\cdot}4}$ c. ft. $= 961{\cdot}5$ c. ft.

$961{\cdot}5$ sq. ft. $= \frac{1}{45}$ of an acre.

∴ the bucket covers $\frac{1}{45}$ of an acre, 1 ft. deep a day.

∴ it covers $\frac{4}{45}$ of an acre, 3 inches in a day.

∴ it covers 1 acre, 3 inches deep in $11\frac{1}{4}$ days.

∴ it covers approximately $2\frac{2}{3}$ acres a month three inches deep.

CHECK.—A well lever here irrigates 4 to 5 Lál Darwázá cottahs of poppy a day, say 10 standard cottahs, and the same land is irrigated every 12 days. ∴ the area commanded by one lever is $\frac{10}{20} \times 12$ of a standard bigha = 6 standard bighas, or about 2 acres.

∴ the area commanded is covered with 3 inches × $2\frac{1}{2}$ ÷ 2 a month = $3\frac{3}{4}$ inches of water per month. ∴ the depth covered at one irrigation is $\frac{15}{4} \times \frac{12}{30} = 1\frac{1}{2}$ inches.

CROSS CHECK.—As $\frac{1}{45}$ of an acre is covered one foot per diem, and as 10 cottahs is roughly $\frac{1}{6}$ of an acre, ∴ the depth of water on land irrigated in one day's work is $\frac{6}{45}$ of a foot, *i.e.*, $1\frac{3}{5}$ inches, which agrees very closely with the above.

The area irrigated by a well lever is materially affected by the distance the water has to be conducted. Thus it is found by experiment that, by conducting water a distance of 150 yards in *kewál* soil (containing about 85 per cent. of clay), the area irrigated in one day is reduced to 5 standard cottahs; that is to say, half the water was lost on the way. The area is also affected by the season of the year. All these experiments refer to the month of November. In February and March the wells begin to dry, and the amount of water raised in the day diminishes.

Poppy land irrigated once every twelve days is taken as the standard.

CASE No. 2.

(*Village Utrend, Pargana Goh.*)

WATER NEAR THE SURFACE.

Depth of well, 2 *porsás,* say 14 ft.
Contents of bucket, $2\frac{1}{2}$ gals.

Number of times raised in half an hour, 140.
Working day = 12 *hours*.

∴ amount of water raised per diem

$= \frac{13 \times 140 \times 2 \times 12}{6} = 7{,}280$ gals.

7,280 gals. = 72,800 lbs. $= \frac{72{,}800}{62 \cdot 4}$ c. ft. = 1,167 c. ft.

1,167 sq. ft. $= \frac{1}{37}$ of an acre.

∴ the bucket covers $\frac{1}{37}$ of an acre, 1 ft. deep in a day.

∴ it covers $\frac{4}{37}$ of an acre, 3 inches deep in a day.

∴ it covers 1 acre, 3 inches deep in 9¼ days.

∴ it covers approximately 3 acres a month 3 inches deep.

CHECK.—A well lever here irrigates (poppy) 4 to 5 L. D. cottahs, say 10 standard cottahs a day, and the same land is irrigated every 12 days. Therefore the area commanded by one lever is $\frac{10}{20} \times 12$ of a standard bigha = 6 bighas, or about 2 acres.

∴ the area commanded in poppy is covered $3 \times 3 \div 2 = 4\frac{1}{2}$ inches in a month. ∴ the depth covered at one irrigation is $4\frac{1}{2} \times \frac{12}{30}$ $= \frac{9}{5}$ inches $= 1\frac{4}{5}$ inches.

CROSS CHECK.—As $\frac{1}{37}$ of an acre is covered one foot per diem, and as 10 cottahs is roughly $\frac{1}{6}$ of an acre, ∴ the depth of water on land irrigated in one day's work is $\frac{6}{37}$ ft. = something under 2 inches, which agrees very closely with the above.

CASE No. 3.

Gaya.

DEEP WELL.

Depth of well, 6 *porsás*, say 40 feet.
Contents of bucket, 2 gals.
Number of times raised in ½ an hour, 90.
Working day = 10 hours.

∴ the amount of water raised per diem

$= 2 \times 90 \times 2 \times 10 = 3{,}600$ gals.

= 36,000 lbs. $= \frac{36{,}000}{62 \cdot 4}$ c. ft. = 576·9 c. ft.

576·9 sq. ft. $= \frac{1}{75}$ of an acre.

∴ the bucket covers $\frac{1}{75}$ of an acre, 1 ft. deep a day.

∴ it covers $\frac{4}{75}$ of an acre, 3 inches in a day.

∴ it covers 1 acre, 3 inches deep in 18¾ days.

∴ it covers approximately 1½ acres a month, 3 inches deep.

Assume that each irrigation of a poppy plot covers the ground 1½ inches, ∴ the area irrigated each day is $\frac{1}{30}$ of 1½ acre ×, $3 \div 1\frac{1}{2} = \frac{1}{10}$ of 3 standard bighas = 6 cottahs.

∴ the area commanded, as each plot is irrigated every 12 days, is 6 × 12 cottahs = 72 cottahs = $3\frac{3}{5}$ standard bighas.

CASE No. 4.

Gaya.

DEEP WELL. LARGE BUCKET.

Depth of well, 44 feet, say 7 *porsás*.

Contents of bucket, 2¼ gals.

Number of times raised in ½ an hour, 93.

Working day = 10 hours.

∴ amount of water raised per diem

$= \frac{9}{4} \times 93 \times 2 \times 10 = 4{,}185$ gals.

$= 41{,}850$ lbs. $= \frac{41{,}850}{62 \cdot 4}$ c. ft. $= 670$ c. ft.

670 sq. ft. $= \frac{1}{65}$ of an acre, approximately.

∴ the bucket covers $\frac{1}{65}$ of an acre, 1 ft. deep a day.

∴ it covers $\frac{4}{65}$ of an acre, 3 inches deep a day.

∴ it covers 1 acre, 3 inches deep in 16¼ days.

∴ it covers something under 2 acres, 3 inches deep in one month.

Assume that each irrigation of a poppy plot covers the ground 1½ inches, ∴ the area irrigated in one day is $\frac{1}{30}$ of 4 acres $= \frac{1}{10}$ of 4 standard bighas = 8 cottahs.

∴ the area commanded, as each plot is irrigated every 12 days, is 8 × 12 cottahs = 96 cottahs = 4 bighas 16 cottahs.

CASE No. 5.

Gaya.

An exceptional case. The workmen were weakly. Well deep.

Depth of well, nominally 5½ *porsás*. Actually 31 ft. 6 inches.

Contents of bucket, 2 gals.

Number of times raised in ½ an hour, 72.

Working day = 10 hours.

∴ amount of water raised per diem

$= 2 \times 72 \times 2 \times 10 = 2{,}880$ gals. $= \frac{28{,}800}{62 \cdot 4}$ c. ft. $= 461 \cdot 5$ c. ft.

461·5 sq. ft. $= \frac{1}{95}$ of an acre.

∴ the bucket covers $\frac{1}{95}$ of an acre, 1 ft. deep in a day.

∴ it covers $\frac{4}{95}$ of an acre, 3 inches deep in a day.

∴ it covers 1 acre, 3 inches deep in 24 days.

∴ it covers approximately 1¼ acre a month, 3 inches deep.

Assume that each irrigation of a poppy plot covers the ground 1½ inches, ∴ the area irrigated each day is $\frac{1}{30}$ of 2½ acres $= \frac{1}{10}$ of 2½ standard bighas = 5 cottahs.

∴ the area commanded, as each plot is irrigated every 12 days, is 5 × 12 cottahs = 60 cottahs = 3 standard bighas, or just one acre.

To sum up.

His Honour the Lieutenant-Governor instituted certain experiments in Darbhanga jail, and found that a well lever could irrigate 2 acres with 3 inches of water per month. The depth of the well is not given, but, judging from Gaya figures, it must have been 35 to 40 feet.

In Gaya we find that, in pargana Goh, the lever of an average well of 20 feet, with a well bucket holding two gallons, and a working day of 12 hours, irrigates $2\frac{1}{2}$ acres a month with 3 inches of water. For poppy the area commanded by a single well lever is about 6 standard bighas, or about 2 acres; and this land is given $1\frac{1}{2}$ inches of water every twelve days.

A well 14 feet deep, with a bucket holding $2\frac{1}{2}$ gallons, irrigates 3 acres a month with 3 inches of water.

A deep well, of say 40 feet, worked 10 hours a day, irrigates $1\frac{1}{2}$ acres (and with a large bucket 2 acres) a month, with three inches of water. If, however, the men who work it are weak or lazy, a well of 30 feet will only irrigate $1\frac{1}{4}$ acres in the same period with the 3 inches of water.

APPENDIX B.

The principal native words used in connexion with irrigation in Gaya district :—

A.—खजाना. *khazáná*, reservoirs.

(1) आहर *áhar*, an *áhar* (*vide* description).

(2) पिण्ड *piṇḍ*, the bank of an *áhar*.

(3) अलंग *alang*, the front, main bank, of an *áhar*.

(4) बँहुआ *bañhuá*, the side banks of an *áhar*.

(5) सिंगा *singá*, the training banks of an *áhar*.

(6) आहर का पेट *áhar ká péṭ*, the bed of an *áhar*.

(7) आहर का पीठ *áhar ká píṭh*, the land in front of the main bank.

(8) कनवह *kanwah*, a safety channel.

(9) खाँड़ *kháñṛ*, a breach or cut in a bank.

(10) खँड़हू *khañṛahú*, the same.

(11) नाली *nálí*, a drain.

(12) टँड़ुआ *ṭañṛuá*, a channel, one to two feet broad and high.

(13) खाँर *kháñr*, the hollow made in the ground by water falling over a sluice.

(14) अहरी *aharí*, a small *áhar*.

(15) पोखर *pókhar*, a tank.

(16) तालाब *táláb*, a tank.

(17) पोखरी *pokhrí*, a small tank.

(18) बावली *báolí*, a small tank.

(19) खंदक *khandak*, a large ditch.

(20) खाता *khátá*, a ditch.

(21) खनित *khanit*, a ditch.

(22) खाई *khái*, a ditch or hollow.

(23) गबड़ा *gabṛá*, a small ditch or hollow.

(24) ढोँगा *ḍhóñgá*, a wooden drain pipe; usually made of a palmyra stem.

(25) गेंड़ा *géñrá*, a *géñṛá*, see explanation.

(26) खँडौत *khanḍaut*, the same as a *géñṛá*.

(27) घेरवा *gherwá*, the outer bank of a *géñṛá*.

(28) किआरी *kiárí*, the square fields in a *géñṛá*.

B.—राह आमद पानी क़ुदर्ती *ráh ámad pání kudartí*, natural sources of water-supply.

(1) बरसन *barsan*, rain-water.

(2) ठाठा *ṭháṭhá* or ठट्ठा *ṭhaṭṭhá*, surface water.

(3) बाहा *báhá*, a natural shallow channel in which surface water collects and is carried away.

(4) नदी *nadí*, a river.

(5) नाला *nálá*, a water-course.

(6) ढोँड़ा *ḍhóñṛá*, a shallow *nálá*, with perpendicular sides.

(7) सोत *sót*, a long shallow *nálá*.

(8) झरना *jharná*, a water-fall.

(9) भूर *bhúr*, a spring.

(10) बम *bam*, a strong spring gushing and spouting up.

(11) टोटा *ṭóṭá*, a small spring ¼″ to ½″ in diameter.

(12) सोइ *sói*, water oozing up, or percolating.

C.—राह आमद पानी मसनुई *ráh ámad pání masnuí*, artificial sources of water-supply.

(1) पइन *pain*, see explanation.

(2) दसिऐनपैन *dasiain pain*, a *pain* serving several villages.

(3) डबूर *ḍabúr* or अहोर *ahór*, a hollow dug in a river bed filled with percolating water.

(4) नरेह *naréh*, a training work, a channel dug in the sand, conducting water from the *ḍabúr*, to the intake of a *pain*.

(5) मुँह *muñh* or मोहाना *mohánà*, the mouth or intake of a *pain*.

(6) भोकला *bhoklá*, a sub-channel, or branch *pain*.

(7) बहरेन *baharain*, the end of a *pain* or *bhoklá*.

(8) पिण्ड *piṇḍ*, a bank.

(9) बाँध *báñdh*, a bank, embankment, dam,

(10) गराँड़ी *garáñṛí*, an embankment across a *pain*.

(11) गूँड़ *gúñṛ* or मोरा *mórá*, fascines used as the foundation of a *garáñṛí*.

(12) खूँटा *khúñṭá*, the posts to which the *gúñṛ* are fastened.

(13) चिपा *chípá*, sods for the *garáñṛí*.

(14) छिलका *chhilká* or चहका *chahká*, a masonry spill dam.

(15) जंघा *janghá*, the parapets of a *chhilká*.

(16) भौंह *bhauñh*, the arched drain running underneath a *chhilká*.

D.—तौर पटावन *taur paṭáwan*, modes of irrigation.

(1) छानन *chhánan* } Irrigation by natural flow of water from field
(2) मेलवान *melwán* } to field; down-hill irrigation.

(3) छीच *chhích*, irrigation by throwing up water from a lower to a higher field; up-hill irrigation.

E.—Well irrigation. See Bihár Peasant Life, pages 200 and ff.

CHAPTER V.

Systems of Cultivating Tenures.

THE description given above of the system of irrigation will prepare the reader for the consideration of cultivating tenures under three heads, viz., tenures of—

(1) those lands which are capable of improvement by the tenant himself, alone, as a small capitalist;

(2) those lands in which the tenant, as a small capitalist, can make some improvements, but in which other improvements must be made, and can only be made by the landlord;

(3) those lands which are not capable of improvement by the tenant as a small capitalist, but which require a large capitalist to make any improvement at all.

In all these the tenant is the cultivator.

The first class can be cultivated by him with the expenditure of small capital.

The second class requires capital expenditure from both tenant and landlord.

The third class requires no capital expenditure from the tenant, but heavy capital expenditure is required from the landlord.

In the first class the tenant can depend entirely on his own exertions for the production of a good crop.

In the second class he is dependent partly on himself and partly on his landlord.

In the third class he is entirely dependent on the actions of his landlord for the production of any crop at all.

Lands of the first class are called *nakdí*, or cash-rent lands.

Lands of the second class are called *paran* lands, a native name for which the writer knows no English equivalent.

Lands of the third class are called *bhaolí*, or produce-rent lands.

The land of the first class may be taken as about 25 per cent. of the cultivated land of the district, of the second class as about 5 per cent., and of the third class as about 70 per cent.* These figures are only approximate. They are not derived from actual measurement, but are based on the experience of the best authorities.

The general system of land tenures in Gaya is called the *bhaolí* system, the name being taken from the tenure on which 70 per cent. of the land is held; but this name has given rise to a most erroneous idea that all land in the district is held on the *metayer* system, and that all rents are paid in kind. This is very far from being the fact. It is a fallacy which must be guarded against, as it is a frequently recurring one.

It is a favourite commonplace of administration in these provinces with those who have had no practical experience of the district, that the *bhaolí* system is a barbarous and exploded one, which is equally fatal to habits of thrift and to methods of improvement. But because a thing is a survival of barbarism it is not necessarily bad. Half the things we meet with in the world of civilization are survivals of barbarism, and are not abandoned on that account. The system cannot be called an exploded one which is in full swing amongst a population of four or five millions. The real test, however, is not whether the system is barbarous and exploded or not, but whether it is good or not.

Regarding its alleged fatal consequences, they are not borne out by the writer's experience. He does not know a more hard-working peasantry than that of Gaya. He has trudged miles and miles over field after field, and has found the tenants to be industrious and thrifty in a way which he could never have expected, considering the heavy rents they as a body have to pay. He has sat for hours amongst groups of villagers, chatting with them about their household affairs, their little quarrels, their marriages, their food, and the thousand-and-one things which make up Bihár rural life, and believes that he may claim to possess some knowledge of their inner feelings and their habits. The

---

* See note to page 54.

assertions as to the evil results of the *bhaolí* system are not based on that kind of knowledge.

The mistaken description is founded, in the writer's opinion, on the erroneous belief above referred to, that the *bhaolí* system, like the *metayer* system, is a system of division of the entire produce of a tenant's holding. This is not the fact. The produce of the *nakdí* lands of a holding is not divided at all, and that of the *paran* lands is only divided once in three years. It is necessary, therefore, to describe in greater detail these three kinds of tenures :—

(1) The *nakdí*.
(2) The *paran*.
(3) The *bhaolí*.

By village custom, each tenant has in his holding a fair proportion of land held on each tenure.

The *nakdí* lands may be classed as ordinary *nakdí*, *shikmí*, and *chakaṭh*. The first require no comment. The tenure is similar to that prevailing in other parts of Bihár. *Shikmí* tenures are very common all over the district, and especially in the large properties of the Tikari Ráj. The word does not mean under-tenure, as elsewhere. In Gaya a *shikmí* tenure means a tenure at cash rents fixed for ever. The principle was laid down by a former Maharája of Tikari, who fixed his tenants' cash rents for ever in *sikká*, or as they are locally called *shikká* rupees. From this word *shikká*, the local use of the word *shikmí* is said to be derived.

Chakaṭh or *chikaṭh* lands are lands temporarily settled at cash rents. The term is specially applied to temporary settlements of waste or uncultivated but culturable lands for limited terms of years, at nominal rents, for the purpose of reclaiming them or bringing them under cultivation. The tenure is governed by the terms of the contract between the parties. The name is, however, frequently used to refer to any *nakdí* tenure which is not *shikmí*.

In *nakdí* lands, the tenant makes his own improvements, and reaps the profit of them. These lands are a direct incentive to thrift and to methods of improvement for every settled *raiyat* in the district. Any person who has camped in Gaya will have noticed how powerfully this incentive works. The cultivation of *nakdí* lands is that of a garden, and the writer has often been astonished at the amount of patient labour and rude ingenuity expended on them by people who are charged with want of thrift and incapability of improvement. As already pointed out, these *nakdí* lands are by no means small in area. They form the lands in which the well-irrigated spring crops—the poppy, the wheat, the mustard, and linseed—are grown. The high unirrigated (*ṭáñṛ*) lands on which spring and autumn crops are grown are also often held on *chakaṭh* tenures. Every spot of land that is capable of improvement by a small capitalist is eagerly taken up and held at *nakdí* rates. In fact, one inconvenience of the Gaya *bhaolí* system is the tendency of the tenants to neglect the true *bhaolí* lands for the better paying *nakdí* ones.

As 70 per cent. of the land is *bhaolí* land proper, it may be argued, with an appearance of fairness, "Here is the advocate of the *bhaolí* system himself admitting that 70 per cent. of the land of Gaya is badly cultivated, simply because it is *bhaolí*." But the inference is not good. To be good, it ought to mean that the tenants could cultivate their *bhaolí* lands as they do their *nakdí* ones, without letting the *nakdí* down from its higher level. But the *bhaolí* lands are such that the tenant cannot cultivate them in this way. He cannot provide the all-necessary water, and the only way to get it is to make the man who can give it—the landlord—depend for his rent directly on the result of giving the water.

The second, or *paran*, class of lands in a tenant's holding, consists of the land devoted to sugarcane. It occupies an intermediate position, and is held on a very peculiar tenure. Sugarcane takes up land for about 14 months, and is an exhausting crop. In two years the same land will support two crops—sugarcane and poppy—the latter of which occupies the ground but for a short time. The land in a village fit for sugarcane is therefore divided by custom into three equal plots, in each of which every tenant has a share. Of the three plots each is in turn year by year planted with sugarcane, poppy, or rice, as the case may be. Each year two plots are held at cash rates, and the tenant gets the benefit of any petty improvements he makes. By the third year a larger expenditure of capital is required, and the landlord, as capitalist, steps in. The principle of rotation demands a rice crop, and the landlord, in return for his expenditure, demands a share in the result of the improvements made by it. He is therefore paid a share of the crop instead of a cash rent. If he makes no expenditure this third year, the sugarcane and poppy of the next two years will be a failure, and hence the tenant insists on the landlord acting as capitalist, and gladly gives a share of the rice crop, as an insurance fee. Such a system of holding is also, it must be admitted, most conducive to habits of thrift and to good husbandry.

We now come to the third class, or *bhaolí* lands proper. These are the lands which bear no crop without water.

In these lands the amount of the crop depends on the amount of irrigation facilities supplied. With no such capital expenditure, the produce is literally and actually none. With moderate expenditure it is fair, and with large expenditure it is bumper. Moreover, the amount of resultant crop increases very rapidly, and in direct proportion with the amount of expenditure. So far as there is certainty in human affairs, so certainly do these results follow.

This capital expenditure takes one form, and one only—that of irrigation. As explained at length in the last chapter, the country is intersected by elaborate series of irrigation channels and embankments, the result of centuries of experiments, and representing an expenditure, in the aggregate, of crores of rupees.

Now a single irrigation channel, or a single embankment, does not benefit one tenant only. It benefits thousands, often belonging to different villages separated miles apart, and it is manifest that the expense of creating or maintaining it cannot be borne by any single tenant. It must be borne by a capitalist, and the only capitalist available is the landlord. Custom has therefore decreed that the *gilandází*, as it is called, shall be made and maintained by the landlord, each tenant paying him his quota of the expense.

But it is found by experience that if a fixed rent is paid to a landlord for this land, the temptation to misappropriate the contributions for *gilandází* is irresistible, and the irrigation is starved. The agreement is therefore so framed that the amount of the contributions and the amount of rent shall alike depend on the amount spent by the landlord on *gilandází*. And as this bears a fixed proportion to the actual produce of the land on which it is spent, the contributions and rent are conveniently contracted for by the tenant giving the landlord, each year, half, or in some cases $\frac{9}{16}$, of the produce as it is reaped. In this way, if the landlord spends nothing, he gets nothing. If he spends a moderate amount he gets a fair return, and if he spends a large amount he gets an exceedingly large return for his capital invested. This is well known, and every wise landlord in Gaya lays out on *gilandází* every pice which he can scrape together. There is no such paying outlet for capital: *gilandází* is the life of the cultivators, and the most profitable speculation possible for the landlords.

This is the history of what is called the *bhaolí* system in Gaya. It will be seen that it differs essentially from the *metayer* system. Every square yard which a tenant can improve is given to him at a cash rent, often fixed for ever, and the land which he cannot improve himself, he holds on terms calculated to compel the only person who can improve it to do his duty. Its name is misleading, an incident of a part of a system giving its name to the whole. Really it is a system admirably adapted to the stage of civilization in which Gaya is, which rears up a sturdy (if somewhat rude) peasantry, holding lands at cash rents fixed for ever, which gives every possible encouragement to thrift and to petty improvements on the part of the cultivator, and which at the same time places at his disposal all the advantages of the large capital required for a complete system of irrigation.

In discussing produce rents it must be noted that only the actual grain is divided. All the straw belongs to the tenant. In cases of dispute the landlord does sometimes claim a share of the straw, but that is only to give trouble to the other side.

Two systems of produce rents are in force—the *baṭái* or *agór baṭái* system, under which the crop is actually divided and the landlord's share made over to him; and the *bhaolí* or *dánábandí* system, in which the amount of the crop is appraised, and the raiyat allowed to take the whole away, being debited with the landlord's share, or with its value.

The methods which were detailed in 1858 by the Commissioner of Patna in a letter to the Board of Revenue, are the same as those now in force, and his description may be quoted here, with a few alterations and additions:—

Under the *baṭái* system, the landlord employs men to watch his share of the crop (hence the system is called *agór baṭái*, from *agorná*, to watch) when it approaches maturity, and, when it is ready, cuts and carries it off himself. More usually, however, at the present day, the whole crop is cut and threshed by the *raiyat* under the superintendence of the *zamindar's* servants, and the produce divided on the threshing-floor.

Under the *dánábandí* system, when the crop is ripe, the *patwári* (more accurately *paṭwárí*) (village accountant), the *gumáshta* (landlord's agent), the *amín* (assessor), the *jaríbkash* (or *kaṭhádhar*) or measurer, a *sális* or arbitrator, a *navísinda* or writer, with the headmen of the village and the *raiyat* himself, proceed to the field in which the crop is growing. The measurer then measures the field with the local pole, and the arbitrator goes round it, and, after a consultation with the assessor and the village officials, estimates the quantity of grain in the crop. If the tenant accepts the estimate, the quantity is entered in the *patwári's* field book (*khasra*) and the matter is considered settled. If the tenant objects, or if the assessor and the arbitrator cannot agree, the fellow-tenants are called in as mediators, and if they fail to convince either party, a test (*partál*) takes place. On behalf of the landlord a portion (usually a quarter of a cottah) of the best part of the field is reaped, and an equal portion of the worst part is reaped on behalf of the tenant. The two portions so reaped are threshed, and the grain weighed. If half a cottah in all is reaped, the weight of the crop in seers gives the number of maunds per bigha. Under any circumstances the whole produce of the field is calculated from the amount weighed and entered in the field-book. The tenant is then at liberty to reap the crop and harvest it whenever it suits his convenience. The *patwári* next prepares a paper called a *behrí*, showing the amount of grain in the possession of the tenant, and the respective shares of the landlord and of the tenant, and sends for the landlord's share, which the tenant either pays in grain or money, as may have been agreed upon. If the agreement is to pay in money, the *gumáshta* writes to the officers of the surrounding villages for the *nirikh* or market rate, which is returned on the back of his letter, and an average rate is then struck.

One point should be noted here. There is no such thing in the district, so far as the writer's experience goes, of any local custom as to the method of realization of produce-rent. It is not the case that one village has a permanent custom of always paying rent by the *baṭái* system, and another village the permanent custom of paying rent by the *dánábandí* system. The method is settled at each crop by mutual agreement. When the two parties quarrel, which is rare, the tenants invariably strive for the *baṭái* system, because it gives them unlimited opportunities for misappropriating the grain in the field before it is divided; and the landlord equally invariably strives for the *dánábandí* system, both because he is better protected against peculation, and because he can try to effect a too high appraisement. In the *dánábandí* system, by common custom, any portion of the crop cut before appraisement is appraised at the high rate of twenty maunds per bigha; so that if the tenant does misappropriate any portion of the standing crop, it is a positive gain to the landlord. This custom is generally adhered to, though it is contrary to the provisions of the Bengal Tenancy Act. A comparison of the advantages and disadvantages of the two methods of realizing produce rents will be given later on.

Assuming that the total amount of the produce has been ascertained either by actual weighment (as in the *baṭái* system), or by appraisement (as in the *dánábandí* system), the method of calculating the landlord's share is a complicated process enough. In order to illustrate it, the writer cannot do better than quote, with a few verbal alterations, from a report written by Mr. A. Ogilvy, Manager of the Tikari estate, in the year 1890.

Mr. Ogilvy describes the procedure in the *baṭái* system, but that in the *dánábandí* system is exactly the same, except that the various shares and allowances are calculated out, instead of being actually weighed. Mr. Ogilvy says:—

"The crops after being threshed and cleaned are then divided. First, the practice of *baṭái* or division differs in almost every village, each of which has its own custom or *lagán*. In some villages more and in some less is given or allowed to landlords, tenants, or labourers. When the crops are cut and the sheaves are being harvested each day, the first deduction is made of *mazdúrí* or labourer's share. This is allowed as a rule at different rates for the two classes of labourers, one for outside labour, and a more favourable rate for the regular village servants.

In some villages the rate allowed is 1 sheaf in 21 for outside coolies and 1 in 16 for village servants, in addition to which they are allowed a daily diet allowance, under the name of *lohrá chhakauṭí*, at the rate of, generally, about enough grain in the ear to give for an outsider 5 seers per day, or for a village servant 16 seers per day. In other villages the rate allowed is as high as one sheaf in eleven to village servants, and more often one in twelve. In one village the rate for outside coolies is as high as one in twelve; but this is an exception. The diet allowance also varies. In some villages each cooly gets 2 seers per day; in others 10 seers for each 21 *bojhás* or sheaves cut; in others about 6 seers per day. In some villages, again, outside coolies get only half the allowance. This diet allowance is made over to the tenant to disburse as he likes, and is considered one of his perquisites. After this the blacksmith, carpenter, dhobí, &c., get their shares, generally as follows:—

1 bojhá to barhí (carpenter),
1 „ to lohár (blacksmith),
½ „ to chamár (leather-worker),
½ „ to hajám (barber),
½ „ to dhobí (washerman),
½ „ to bháṭ (village bard),

from each tenant, and to any beggars contributions are given at the rate of ½ seer or one seer each. This last is called *bhichchhá*. After this the remaining sheaves are threshed and the grain collected into one heap and weighed; then out of the undivided grain the village officials are allowed their share (*rasúm*) in the shape of in each maund to the—

Patwári (accountant)	...	...	4 chitaks (*i.e.* 8 oz.)
Gorait (watchman)	...	...	2 „
Baráhil (peon)	...	...	2 „
Kumhár (potter)	...	...	1 chitak.
Ṭahlú (office servant)	...	...	1 „

In some villages the *patwári* and *gumáshta* (landlord's agent) get 8 chitaks between them. The *baráhil*, *gorait*, *haṭwe* (weighman), *ṭahlú* and *kumhár* each 2 chitaks. These allowances are made out of the undivided grain, and thus fall equally on landlord and tenant. In some villages the *badhwár* or field-watcher gets 2 chitaks. In one or two villages I have found 4 chitaks deducted as *chalsá*, which is a perquisite of the landlord, and 4 chitaks as *partúl*, which is a perquisite of the *haṭwe* or weighman. The concessions to the tenants are then made; sometimes under the name of *charserí* or *doserí*, under which 4 seers in one maund are allowed to high castes and two seers to lower castes, or two seers only to higher castes and one seer to lower; sometimes under the name of *tarhí gár* and *bishunpirit*, when a portion of the heap, estimated at about two seers to each maund, is portioned off for the tenant. Then the remaining grain is divided equally between the tenant and landlord; and finally, the concession to the landlord under the name of *neg* at the rate of, on the average, 1¼ seer per maund to each high class, and 2½ seers to each lower class tenant, are deducted from the tenant's heap and given over to the proprietor's heap. These rates differ in each village; there are often three and four classes, the Jeṭhraiyats (or headmen) being most favoured, the lower castes the least; Goálás who supply milk and ghí in some villages are charged a lower rate. In some villages *changí* is charged at the rate of 2½ seers for each 21 *bojhás* or sheaves cut by outside coolies. And again *paserá* at the rate of 5 seers per tenant whose grain exceeds 10 maunds (in some villages 5 maunds is the limit) is also transferred to the proprietor's heap. Finally, from the proprietor's heap the gorait gets a *pabbí* of 4 chitaks per maund, and the Gauñwa Páṇḍe or village priest another 4 chitaks. On taking an average of 5 villages I have found that the average cost of labour of cutting comes to from 8·8 to 7·9 per cent., and that of the balance, after deducting 2·4 per cent. for the village officials, the tenant gets 49·16 to 48 per cent. according to his caste, and the landlord 48 to 49·66 per cent.; in other words, that, granted the sharing of the portions of the village officials, the landlords and tenants as a practice divide half and half, the lower castes getting rather less, and the favoured castes rather more. As to whether the village officials' shares should be deducted equally from the tenant's as from the landlord's shares, there is a good deal to be said on both sides. The village officials, though nominally the servants of the landlord, are in this district required quite as much by the tenant as by the landlord, and their services are utilised for the benefit of both; the patwári, who takes the largest share, is really the village solicitor. The tenants are all illiterate men, and are, as a rule, dependent upon the patwári for their titles to any property they possess,—certainly for their titles in land. He writes any deeds that are required in the village, and acts as scribe generally to the community. The gumáshta has the responsibility of the irrigation of the crops, and has to settle disputes between the different tenants as to water, &c. He also heads the villagers when they have to protect their rights by a *levée en masse*, and also in the subsequent inevitable litigation. The baráhils are expected by the tenants to watch the crops and prevent grazing. The ṭahlú and kumhár seem to be engaged more in the landlord's interest than the tenant's, but they are appurtenances of the patwári and gumáshta and, as such, their share must be taken along with the patwáris and gumáshtas.

It is thus found that the landlord and tenant both make concessions to each other, and that as a result the landlord only receives about

$\frac{7\frac{1}{4}}{16}$ of the gross produce, out of which he has to pay the tithes of the village priests; so that as a nett result he receives only $\frac{7\frac{7}{40}}{16}$ of the produce. This is very much less than is usually assumed to be the case, and shows that under conditions in which neither party can dispense with the assistance of the other, they can manage their affairs very well by themselves. The concessions to the tenant do not extend to the small portion of the cultivation that is covered by fixed cash rents; at any rate they are not so apparent, although the higher castes very often pay a smaller rent than the lower, and do not make the same contribution towards the pay of the patwári and village establishment.

The natural result of this very complicated system is that when a landlord is non-resident, or has more than merely one or two villages, he is obliged, for his own protection, to lease them out to *ṭhíkedárs* or farmers, who take on themselves the onus of the fluctuation in production, and the difficulties in realizing the rental. The reason of this is not far to seek. Under a system of fixed cash rental, the proprietor knows quite well what he has to receive from each village, and can without very much trouble assure himself against peculation in its collection. But when the rental is a fluctuating one, depending on the amount of the crop, it may be anything. It may be forty per cent. less than, and it may be forty per cent. more than, the normal amount; and although great and unexplained fluctuations may be guarded against and the responsibility of the village officials in regard to them enforced, it is impossible for the landlord to know with certainty if fluctuations of a few points on either side of the normal are correctly accounted for or not.

The village officials either appraise the crops or divide them with the tenants. In the former case, owing to the fact that the crops can only be judged when ripe, the appraisement has to be done so quickly, and the harvesting, to prevent deterioration, must be carried out so promptly, that a proprietor cannot check it himself, in more than one or two villages, beyond estimating whether the total appraisement is a satisfactory result for the season.

If it is not, he may send some one else, or he may go himself to make a fresh appraisement. If his property be so small that he can himself carry out this checking, then he may escape becoming a victim to the facilities which the system opens to peculation; but, on the other hand, if the property be one that obliges him to depend upon his servants for this check, then he can have no assurance whatever. Most small proprietors call in the assistance of their relatives to help at the time of appraisement, but, the writer has been informed by many, they can never trust even them. The temptation to peculation is too great, and there is practically no chance of detection.

When the crops are divided on the threshing-floor, under the *baṭaí* system, the local establishment is even more powerfulf or evil, as here there is no possibility of check as there is with an appraisement. The grain is divided as it is harvested, or as it is threshed, and until the whole crop has been finished, the proprietor has no guide as to what the general result will be. When this result is put before him, it is too late to recover any of the grain which has been made away with, and practically impossible to trace it; for the tenants, sharing the results of peculation with the village establishment, are interested in concealing what has occurred.

Unless, therefore, the landlord of a large estate is a very active man, and unless he has a sufficient number of subordinates, sufficiently highly paid to make it worth their while to be trustworthy, he is compelled to lease out each village to a petty local capitalist, who will pay him a fixed sum in cash every year for the right of collecting the produce rental. This system is the one which has been in force even in large well-managed estates like the Tikari Ráj. Not even the Mahárájás who have left behind them a great name for energy in the supervision of their estates have ever attempted direct management for any length of time; though they never scrupled to interpose, when necessary, a strong arm between the farmer and the tenant, and to exercise a clear judgment in protecting the weaker side and putting down oppression.

It has been found, however, by experience in the Court of Wards' and Government estates in this district, that direct management of *bhaolí* estates is not only possible, but profitable, if the manager is energetic and has sufficient well-paid subordinates. The example set by Government is being taken up by other large landholders, and now the Rájá of Maksúdpur is managing his fine estates on the same principle, with, the writer believes, great profit to himself.

On the other hand, it must be noted that, as will subsequently be shown, the farming system in Gaya is robbed of most of its objectionable features by the necessity of the farmer remaining on good terms with the tenants, and also by the fact that as a rule the same family of farmers holds the same village generation after generation. He lives on the spot, amongst the tenants, is one of themselves, and is amenable to public opinion. It is not till the term of his farming lease approaches its conclusion, and he loses hope of its renewal, that, impelled by greed of gain, he neglects the *gilandází*, and screws all that he can out of his unhappy tenants. In such cases custom most beneficially allows the head landlord to interfere.

The farmer, it is unnecessary to state, has hitherto annexed a very large proportion of the rental as his profit. He has first to be paid for his undertaking the risks incident to fluctuating receipts, while he pays a fixed rent himself to the landlord. He also charges highly for relieving the landlord of the consequences of the dishonesty of his servants, and the landlord willingly pays a heavy sum for this. Al these farmer's profits are saved by direct, or as it is called *sir*, management. Under the latter system the landlord inevitably loses something by peculation: but, if he manages well, that loss will be, on the average of a series of years, nothing like what he would have paid to the farmer.

A few more remarks on this system may be added. One is that it has produced an abnormal power of judging crops amongst the inhabitants of the district. The habit of constant appraisement enables any countryman or scion of a landlord's or farmer's house to go into a field, pluck a few ears of corn, and say, "The crop in this field is so many maunds a bigha." If he is not intentionally seeking to mislead, a test will show that his estimate is certain to be wonderfully correct. To a native of another district this power seems to be something uncanny. He does not grasp that it is simply the result of practice.

Another point to be noticed is the fact that, almost alone in the province, the district of Gaya shows an Indian people with real landlords; that is to say, a body of rent receivers, who are not simply annuitants burdening the estate, but who take a lively interest in the welfare of their tenants.

Whether he is a direct managing landlord or a farmer with a lease to run, the rent-receiver has to work in common with the tenant to raise their joint crop. The relations therefore of landlord (under which term is here included the farmer) and cultivating tenant are much more cordial than elsewhere. The landlord is dependent on the tenant, because his rental depends upon the produce which results from the tenant's labour; and if the latter were, from any disaffection to the landlord, to hold his hand and desist altogether from cultivation, the income of the former would disappear. It is true that he might recover damages from the tenant, but that is a slow and uncertain revenge; while, if the tenant, instead of abstaining from all cultivation, simply cultivates badly with the object of spoiling the outturn, the landlord will have no redress, and is entirely at his mercy.

To such an extent does this dependence upon the loyalty of the tenant affect the relations of the parties, that, were it not for an equal dependence of the tenant upon the landlord for irrigation works, the tenant would be in a position to ride roughshod over the former, and to dictate terms as he pleased. The necessity, however, of placing the control of the irrigation of the village in the hands of a person paramount, such as the landlord, and the inability of the tenants either to combine to meet the expense of the common irrigation works, or to divide impartially the benefits of any works that may be affected, throw them back upon the landlords, and thus restores to the latter the authority of which in other ways the *bhaolí* system deprives them. As a matter of practice the harmony of their relations is but seldom turned to discord. People without experience of the district are struck by the very small number of rent suits instituted in the civil courts, and theorists have even reported that this is due to the fact of the helplessness of the tenants, which allows the landlords to do what oppression they please. But the reverse is the fact. Nowhere else in the province are the relations of landlord and tenant so amicable as they are in Gaya, and this is not because the people have a smaller dose of original sin than elsewhere, but because self-interest prevents the landlords from overstepping certain well-understood limits of authority, and compels them to take an active interest in the welfare of their tenants, while the same motive power urges the tenants to keep on good terms with their landlords, without whom their very existence would be difficult. Each side is necessary to the existence of the other, and each side knows it.

In this connexion, the question of *abwábs* may be alluded to. Under the Tenancy Act their collection is illegal; yet, as will have been noticed above (pp. 75 and ff), in the description of the method of division of crops, a number of unauthorized payments, of uncertain amount, are made to the landlord, in addition to his rent proper. These are almost certainly *abwábs*, as prohibited in the Tenancy Act, but no tenant ever dreams of disputing them.

These allowances to the landlord are concessions which in other districts, where the landlord has the tenant at his mercy, are mere exactions and enhancements of rent in disguise. But in Gaya, where the landlord is, on the contrary, dependent on the continuance of amicable relations with his tenants, they are little more than practices of courtesy passing between the two persons concerned. The landlord makes concessions to the tenant, and the tenant makes the same to the landlord. The Tenancy Act, aiming at abuses occurring elsewhere, has condemned the latter concessions as illegal and arbitrary, while it takes no heed of concessions to the tenant. As, however, the conditions of agriculture in Gaya forbid any disagreement between landlord and tenant, the practice of making concessions on both sides continues in full force, and the effect of the Tenancy Act in this respect has been practically *nil*.

To sum up the question of the advantages and disadvantages of the *bhaolí* system.

Its advantages are, that without it the tenant would get no water, and that hence 70 per cent. of the cultivated area of the district would be thrown out of cultivation.

It does not affect those lands which the tenant can improve himself, and hence it does not discourage habits of thrift, or lead to slovenly cultivation.

It compels the landlords (including farmers) to be landlords indeed, and not mere annuitants.

It successfully tends to keep up the most amicable relations between landlord and tenant.

Its disadvantages are the following:—

It is expensive to manage, and makes the existence of middlemen almost a necessity. Owing, however, to the circumstances of the tenure, the middleman cannot press the tenants beyond certain well-defined limits.

It opens wide doors to peculation, especially when large estates are managed direct, and in such cases requires highly paid establishments to keep down this peculation within moderate limits.

Finally, in comparing cash and produce rents, the writer's experience has led him to the conclusion that, *cœteris paribus*, the former are a good deal lower than the latter. That is to say, if the cash rent of a piece of land were a hundred rupees, the average value of the produce rent of the same piece, calculated on a number of years, would probably be a hundred and twenty or a hundred and thirty.

This is only what is reasonable. With a cash rent, the tenant undertakes all the risks of fluctuations of crops, due to vicissitudes of the seasons, and insures a regular fixed rent every year to the landlord. With a produce rent, the landlord takes half the risk, spends large sums on providing irrigation, and has to keep up an expensive establishment to watch the crop. The tenant, too, has his rent tempered according to his circumstances, and in consideration of this convenience is prepared to pay a larger average sum.

In conclusion, the table of agricultural operations given opposite will be found interesting and useful. Agriculture in Gaya follows the position of the sun amidst the lunar asterisms, and thus follows the solar and not the luni-solar year. The table shows the weather which the most experienced cultivators consider most advantageous for each crop, asterism by asterism.

CHAPTER VI.

The Productive Powers of the Soil.

FOR the purposes of discussing the productive powers of the soil of Gaya, it is necessary to divide the district into four tracts more or less compact, as illustrated in the accompanying map.

The first, or *fertile*, tract is the Jahanabad subdivision, and the Western Canal irrigated strip of the Aurangabad subdivision, consisting of Jahanabad and Arwal thánas, and of a portion of Daudnagar thána or of parganas Ikkil, Bheláwar, Okrí, Arwal, and a portion of Siris.

The western portion of this tract has the benefit of canal irrigation, while the northern and eastern portions are intersected by *pains* or irrigation channels leading from the rivers Morhar and Mubáná. Moreover, the greater part of this portion of the district was once the basin of the Sone river itself, and the soil is largely composed of old alluvial deposit, and is naturally more productive than that of other portions of the district.

The second, or *moderately* fertile, tract consists of two areas, the first being composed of thánas Gaya, Tikari, and Atari in the centre of the district, and the second of thána Nabinagar in the extreme south-west. The corresponding parganas are Sanaut, Pahrá, Atari, a portion of Narhaṭ, Kábar, and Dakhner for the first, and Kuṭumbá for the second. These areas have also the benefit of ample irrigation from several rivers, and there are very few villages which have not either a *pain* or a *bhoklá* (sub-channel) from some efficient source of water-supply.

The third, or *less fertile*, tract also consists of two areas, the first being the Nawádah subdivision, consisting of thánas Nawádah, Pakribarwan, and Rajauli; and the second the rest of the Aurangabad subdivision, consisting of thána Aurangabad and of a portion of thána Daudnagar. The corresponding parganas are (1) Samai, Roh, Jarrab, a portion of Narhaṭ, Charkáwáñ, and (2) Siris and others. Only about half the villages in these two areas are sufficiently irrigated, and moreover, the *pains* that do exist only give an adequate supply of water in years of good rainfall.

The fourth, or *infertile*, tract consists of thánas Sherghati and Barachati, or the southern half of the Sadar subdivision. It is nearly all contained in Sherghati pargana. Besides containing extensive tracts of *jangal*, there are few *pains*, and only about ten per cent. of the villages are irrigated. Hence paddy is little cultivated, as compared with the rest of the district, and where it is cultivated it is liable to total failure in a moderately bad year.

Before dealing with these tracts one by one, it will be convenient to consider the classes of land according to the crops they bear. Broadly speaking, land may be divided into paddy, *rabi*, and sugarcane land. The last crop occupies the ground for some thirteen or fourteen months, and hence sugarcane land only bears one crop in the year.

Paddy land may be divided into two classes. The first comprises the sandy soils known as *paurú* and as *rèhrá*; the second the clay soil known as *kewál*. The former bear only one crop—paddy—in a single year; the latter bears a second crop in the spring, such as *khesárí*, gram, &c. The paddy lands may therefore be considered as bearing either paddy only, or as bearing paddy and *khesárí*.

The *rabi* lands may again be divided into two classes, those which bear cereals only, and those which bear an autumn (*bhadoī*) crop as well. The *bhadoí* crop consists of *maruá*, *kodo*, Indian-corn, sixty-day rice, and other less important grains. A certain proportion of the best land of the second class, especially of those near the village sites, is devoted to poppy instead of cereals.

We thus get the following classification:—

1. Paddy lands ... *a.* Paddy only.
   b. Paddy and *khesárí*.
2. Rabi lands ... *a.* Cereals only.
   b. Cereals and *bhadoí*.
   c. Poppy and *bhadoí*.
3. Sugarcane lands.

Owing to the peculiar nature of the soil requisite for poppy, the outturn of poppy lands is pretty constant all over the district, and may be taken to average six standard seers of opium, two local maunds of poppy-seed and six local maunds of *bhadoi* per opium bigha; that is to say, 9·6 standard seers, 2 standard maunds, and 6·2 standard maunds per acre respectively. Similarly, sugarcane may be taken as producing 25 local maunds of molasses per local bigha (25·5 standard maunds per acre) throughout the district. Five per cent. of the cultivated land in all four tracts may be taken as devoted to poppy, and 5 per cent. in the first and second tracts, 4 per cent. in the third tract, and 3 per cent. in the fourth tract, as devoted to sugarcane.

Having thus cleared the way by disposing of poppy and sugarcane, we may proceed to consider the paddy and the *rabi* lands in each tract separately. The following figures may be taken as representing what in other parts of the province would be considered as fourteen-anna crops. They represent the averages of several years, good and bad taken together.

For the first, or fertile, tract the statistics upon which we have to go consist of (1) the appraisement of the large Government estate of Ghenjan in the year 1881, which was a good paddy year, and in which the average outturn of paddy per local bigha was found to be 7·8 local maunds. In the following year (which was not such a good one) the average outturn of three other villages was 5·6 maunds. The village papers for the three years (1293, 1294, and 1295 F.S.) of three other fairly typical villages in the same tract, the property of a private landlord, give an average of 10·5 maunds per bigha. The figures for the *sir* villages of the Tikari ward's estate for the year 1294 F.S., which was a bad year, do not exceed 5·3 maunds, while the road cess returns for three years give 7·3 maunds. The last average, however, includes also the *rabi* outturn, which was much smaller, and the road cess returns of paddy alone would have been larger.

Taking all these facts, and the areas and localities of the villages selected, into consideration, the writer is of opinion that the highest estimate at which we can put the average outturn in the whole fertile tract of an average paddy crop, is 10·5 local maunds per local bigha, or 10·8 standard maunds per acre.

As regards the *rabi* crops (including *khesári*, which although grown on *kewál* paddy land, is really a *rabi* crop), the figures of the private zamindar already alluded to give an average outturn of 4·3 maunds per bigha. The appraisements for 1881 give only 3·2 maunds. The Court of Wards' figures give 3·9 maunds, and those for Ghenjan for the years for 1886-87 and 1887-88 give an average of 5 maunds a bigha. Independent estimates of native experts give the average *rabi* outturn for the tract at about 5 maunds per bigha, and we may accept this figure as a maximum, it being partially borne out by the others just recorded. We may therefore take it that in an average year the average outturn of *khesári* and *rabi* in the fertile tract is 5 local maunds per local bigha, or 5·1 standard maunds per acre. This will give 15·5 local maunds per local bigha (15·9 standard maunds per acre) as the average produce of land under both paddy and *khesári*, and 11 local maunds per local bigha (11·8 standard maunds per acre), for land under both *rabi* and *bhadoi*, the outturn of the latter being 6 maunds a bigha. The *bhadoi* crop not being important, it is unnecessary to give in detail the figures which lead to this result.

The figures already quoted show that the percentage of simple paddy land in this first tract is 25, and of paddy and *khesári* lands 20. That of simple *rabi* is 40 and of *rabi* and *bhadoi* 5.

For the second, or moderately fertile tract, more figures are available. There are a large number of Government estates within it, with valuation papers going back as far as the year 1880. There are also figures of the Tikari ward's estate for 1294 F.S., and the road cess papers filed during a late revaluation. Omitting details,* the average outturn

* The following figures regarding paddy are the average of two years 1886-87 and 1887-88 in certain Government estates:—

Name of Estate.			*Average outturn in local maunds per local bigha.*
Dakhner	...	...	9
Utrend-Páli	...	...	8·5
Bardi Maniárá	...	...	8

In 1880, which was a good paddy year, the figures were—

Name of Estate.			*Outturn in local maunds per local bigha.*
Utrend	...	...	8·3
Páli	...	...	7·1
Simuárá	...	...	7
Goharpur	...	...	12·2
Pachambá	...	...	6·4

of paddy in an average year in this second tract may be estimated at 8·5 local maunds per local bigha (8·6 standard maunds per acre).

The average rabi outturn is 3·9 local maunds per bigha (4 standard maunds per acre);* the average outturn of lands under both paddy and *khesárí* is therefore 8·5 + 3·9, say 12·5 local maunds per local bigha (12·8 standard maunds per acre).

The outturn of the *bhadoí* crop was found to vary between 7·9 maunds to 5·5 maunds per bigha, according to locality. The crop is an addition to the *rabi* crop on the same land, and is of small importance. The average outturn was about 6 local maunds per local bigha (6·2 standard maunds per acre). The total outturn of the double-cropped land is therefore 6·2+4 = 10·2 standard maunds an acre.

In this tract 45 per cent. of the cultivated area was found to be under paddy alone, 10 per cent. under paddy and *khesárí*, 30 per cent. under *rabi* alone, and 5 per cent. under *rabi* and *bhadoí*.

For the third, or less fertile, area trustworthy figures from numerous Government estates are also forthcoming. In the irrigated villages, the outturn of paddy varies in average years between 7⅛ and 8⅓ maunds. The other villages, being entirely dependent on the rainfall, in a good year produce much more, and in a bad year nothing at all. The result is, therefore, that the average outturn of all paddy lands in this tract is 7 local maunds per bigha (7·2 standard maunds per acre). The average outturn of *khesárí* and of *rabi* is about the same as that of the second tract, the soil being similar, and the crops not being so dependent on irrigation. It is therefore 3·9 local maunds per local bigha (4 standard maunds per acre). The soil being drier, the area under *khesárí* and simple *rabi* is larger (12 per cent. and 32·5 per cent., respectively), but that under *rabi* and *bhadoí* is less, being only 2½ per cent. of the whole cultivated area.

The fourth, or infertile, tract varies greatly. When a village is lucky enough to have a *pain*, the produce of paddy is on an average 7 maunds a bigha. The figures of mahál Saráñwáñ, which has no *pain*, show an average of 5 maunds a bigha. The average paddy outturn of this tract may be estimated at 6 maunds per local bigha (6·2 standard maunds an acre); the figures for *rabi* and *khesárí* are pretty steady over the whole area, and average 3 maunds a local bigha (3 standard maunds an acre).

---

* The average of Utrend-Páli for 1886-87 and 1887-88 gives 6·1 maunds per bigha; of Bardi Maniárá 3·9 maunds. In 1880 the following were the figures:—

Name of Estate.			*Outturn in local maunds per local bigha.*
Simuárá	...	...	2·6
Goharpur	...	...	
Pachambá	...	...	
Utrend-Páli	...	...	2·9
Dakhner	...	...	3·3

Rabi and *bhadoi* are much more cultivated in this unfertile tract than elsewhere in the district.

The following table gives the result of this inquiry in a tabular form:—

Name of crop.	Percentage of the area under the crop to the total area cultivated.				Average outturn of the crops in local maunds and local bighas.				Average outturn of the crops in standard maunds and acres.			
	First tract.	Second tract.	Third tract.	Fourth tract.	First tract.	Second tract.	Third tract.	Fourth tract.	First tract.	Second tract.	Third tract.	Fourth tract.
Paddy	25	45	44	37	10·5	8·5	7·0	6	10·8	8·6	7·2	6·2
Do. and khesári	20	10	12	10	15·5	12·5	10·6	9	15·9	12·8	11·2	9·2
Rabi	40	30	32·5	35	5·0	3·9	3·9	3	5·1	4·0	4·0	3·0
Bhadoi and rabi ...	5	5	2·5	10	11	10	10	9	11·3	10·2	10·2	9·2
Do. and poppy ...	5	5	5	5	6 maunds *bhadoi*, 6 seers* opium, 2 maunds poppy seed.				6·2 maunds *bhadoi*, 9·6 seers opium, 2 maunds poppy seed.			
Sugarcane	5	5	4	3	25				25·6			

* Opium is given in standard seers.

It is not improbable that these estimates may be considered to be very low, but the writer does not consider that as averages of the average outturns of a number of years they can be put higher. No doubt there are many fortunate villages, in the canal-irrigated tracts, which give as much as 25 maunds of paddy an acre; but these are few, and are counterbalanced by the many fields which, except in a good year, give nothing at all. In support of the figures, it may be recorded that some years ago the Rájá of Tikari, when managing his estates *sir*, found on one occasion that the average of his paddy harvest was 10 local maunds per local bigha (10¼ standard maunds per acre), and that the occasion was deemed worthy of special rejoicing.

Since then the estate has been under the Court of Wards, and has been greatly improved. Cultivation is now more successful, owing to increased facilities for irrigation. The *Faslí* year 1288 (1890-91 A.D.) was a year of exceptionally good rainfall, and full statistics of the different assessments for that year are available in the manager's office. Bearing in mind that they are figures of an exceptionally good year, they confirm the statistics given above in a remarkable way. Thirty-eight thousand one hundred and sixty different assessments of the rice crop, covering 14,281 acres, were made, and the gross outturn was 1,90,463 standard maunds, being an average of 13 maunds 13 seers 7 chitaks per acre.

The manager of the estate remarks regarding these figures:—"This is in a good year. In the present year (1891-92) the produce is likely to be only about one quarter of that of last year, say 3½ maunds per acre. I daresay that the average may be estimated at 9 to 9½ maunds per acre."

The *rabi* figures for 1890-91 for *kewál* soil in the same estate are as follows:—

	Maunds per acre. Mds.	Srs.
Masurí (vetch)	5	34
Linseed	4	9
Kerao (pease)	6	9
Rhesárí	3	11 7/16
Gram	4	27 2/16
Wheat	4	37 7/16
Barley	6	4 8/16
Ráhar	2	33 15/16
Wheat and gram mixed ...	4	13
Wheat and barley mixed ...	5	23 8/16
Gram and barley mixed ...	9	21

Thirty-one thousand nine hundred and seventy-eight appraisements in 14,546 acres, gave a gross outturn of 68,853 maunds, or an average of 4 maunds and 29 seers 4½ chitaks per acre, and this, too, in a good year.

The same year was a bad one for *bhadoi* crops, and hence the following figures (for *kewál* land) are much below the average:—

	Mds.	Srs.
Maruá	3	19
Sixty-day rice	4	30
Kodo	2	25
Urid	1	20
Makai	1	11
Kurthí	3	29

One thousand six hundred and twenty-three appraisements in 596 acres, gave a gross outturn of 2,212 maunds, or an average of 3 maunds 28 seers 6 chitaks per acre.

The manager further remarks:—"The outturn of the double crop paddy fields is shown to be 13 maunds 13 seers 7 chitaks for paddy, and 3 maunds 11 seers 7 chitaks for *khesárí*, or altogether 16 maunds 24 seers 14 chitaks per acre. This is for a good year. In a year like the present (1891-92), the *khesárí* outturn is nil, and the paddy about 3½ maunds or 4 maunds per bigha. The average of good and bad years may be taken as 11½ maunds per acre."

CHAPTER VII.

On The Poorer Classes of the District.

DIVIDING the poorer classes into four orders—cultivators, agricultural labourers, artizans, and those who subsist on charity—it has been found from a census of over 10,000 people, held in the year 1888, that, roughly speaking, one-half consists of the first class, one-fourth of each of the second and third, and a very small fraction consists of the fourth. The exact figures are 53·0 per cent., 23·0 per cent., 23·8 per cent., and 0·2 per cent., respectively.*

These figures require explanation, for the border line between cultivators and labourers is not very clearly defined. Under labourers are included those who, like *kamiyás* in certain portions of the district, have a small plot of land, but who live mainly by unskilled field labour. Under the head of cultivators are included those who live mainly on the profits of small holdings assisted by the wages of labour. If we separate from these two classes those who live by pure labour and those who live by labour and agriculture combined, it has been found from actual counting of the inhabitants of ten selected villages in the Jahánabad subdivision that 197 families, numbering 841 members, depended entirely on the labour of 407 persons, while 2,056 persons subsist on labour wages plus the profits of 171 small holdings ranging in area from a few poles to 10 acres. The average area of these holdings is 2 roods 25 poles. Taking, therefore, the whole number of persons in these villages who subsist wholly or in part on the wages of labour, about 29 per cent. of them have no additional income from land, while 71 per cent. have.

On the whole, the first division given is the most useful, for it divides the agricultural community into two broad classes, viz., those who live wholly or mainly by cultivating their own land, and those who live wholly or mainly by cultivating other people's land. The former are called cultivators and the latter labourers.

---

* The following figures give fuller details, subdivision by subdivision, for three subdivisions. The figures obtained for Nawádah subdivision are omitted, as the writer was not able to satisfy himself that they were approximately correct:—

Name of sub-division.	Population counted.	Cultivators.		Agricultural labourers.		Artizans.		Dependent on charity.		Remarks.
		Number.	Percentage.	Number.	Percentage.	Number.	Percentage.	Number.	Percentage.	
Sadar	2,075	939	45·3	641	30·8	495	23·3	...	...	Note that the proportion of cultivators in the fertile tracts of Jahánabad is larger than elsewhere.
Aurangabad ...	1,844	781	42·3	339	18·3	708	38·3	16	0·8	
Jahánabad ...	6,714	3,907	58·2	1,473	21·9	1,324	19·7	10	0·1	
District total ...	10,633	5,627	53·0	2,453	23·0	2,527	23·8	26	0·2	

The heading of artizans requires some slight correction, as it includes other non-cultivating villagers, such as traders, priests and landlords, who do not cultivate in the village. The number of these is, however, very small, and may be neglected in dealing with the question practically.

A census of thirteen villages, with 732 families of 4,674 persons, shows that the average number of persons in a family is 6·3. If all the members of a family are dependent on the wages of labour, they are all classed as labourers, even though some may be children and do not work. So all the members of a cultivator's family are classed as cultivators, and of an artizan's family as artizans. This classification is obviously the only possible one.

Taking the whole poorer population of the district, and excluding infants in arms, it is found by a number of independent calculations that the cost of living, including food, salt, tobacco, pottery, &c., and clothing, is about Rs. 15 per head per annum, supposing each member of the family gets his two full meals a day. Anything less than this means a corresponding reduction in food or clothing or both. Speaking more accurately, a family of six persons should spend Rs. 93, and a family of four persons Rs. 61-12 per annum, if each member gets two meals a day and has moderate comforts.*

---

* The following are the calculations:—

A.—A family of six persons—

	Seers.
(1) Two adult males, each taking two meals of ¾ seer of rice at each meal, equal to 3 seers of rice or 4½ seers of paddy.	4½
(2) One adult female, taking two meals of ½ seer of rice at each meal, equal to 1 seer of rice or 1½ seers of paddy.	1½
(3) Three children, each taking ½ seer of rice per diem, equal to 1½ seers of rice or 2¼ seers of paddy.	2¼
(4) Pulses for the family	1¾
Total ...	10 seers per diem.

Ten seers per diem equal 73 maunds (at a rupee a maund) annually. To this add Rs. 12 for salt, tobacco, pottery, &c., and Rs. 8 for clothing. Total Rs. 93.

B.—A family of four persons—

	Seers.
(1) One adult male as above	2¼
(2) One adult female as above	1½
(3) Two children as above	1½
(4) Pulses for the family	1
Total ...	6¼ seers per diem.

Six and a quarter seers per diem equal 45 maunds annually, costing Rs. 45. To this add Rs. 10 for salt, tobacco, pottery, &c., and Rs. 6-12 for 40 yards of coarse cloth. Total Rs. 61-1.

Common rice is eaten for the principal meal of the day. The cost of other grains, if eaten, is about the same, so that, expressed in rupees, the result is not altered whatever grain is taken.

M

The seers and maunds given in the foot-note are local weight. The local seer referred to is about 50* Company's tolás in weight. In estimating a man's food at 1½ seers of rice plus a share of pulse, he is therefore given 75 standard tolás of rice plus about 21 tolás of pulse, *i.e.*, 96 tolás altogether, or about 19 chitaks. The Bihár jail allowance for labouring prisoners (18 chitaks, excluding oil and spices) is slightly less than this; but it must be remembered that in a jail large numbers are dealt with and averages can be taken. In a cultivator's or labourer's family the number is too small for an average to be struck, and a margin must be allowed. In a jail, too, regular hours of meals, good house accommodation, sanitary precautions, freedom from exposure to the sun, proper medical treatment and dietary in illness,—all these permit the allowance of food to be safely brought down lower than outside.

*More accurately about 52. The *seer* of course varies in almost every bazar, but the 52-tola *seer* is the one most commonly met with.

A local maund of paddy may, for purposes of calculation, be taken as being equal to one rupee. It varies in price, according to season, between 6 and 10 local *paserís*, there being 8 *paserís* to the maund.

CHAPTER VIII.

Area of Cultivators' Holdings.

THE average area of a holding all over the district is about 16 local bighas, or 10 acres. It varies according to locality. For instance, in the south-west of the district, where there is much *táñr* or high unirrigated land, it averages 20 local bighas, or 12½ acres.

The following figures refer to 3,649 holdings, and were obtained from every portion of the district:—

SIZE OF HOLDINGS.				Percentage of whole number.
LOCAL BIGHAS.		ACRES.		
Above.	Up to and including.	Above.	Up to and including.	
...	5	...	3⅛	48·5
5	10	3⅛	6¼	21·7
10	20	6¼	12½	17·4
20	50	12½	31¼	10·4
50	100	31¼	62½	1·5
100	200	62½	125	·1
200	and over	125	and over.	·02

From the above it will be seen that 70 per cent. of the cultivators have holdings of 10 local bighas (6¼ acres) and under, and 87 per cent. of the cultivators have holdings of 20 bighas (12½ acres) and under.

In the following statement the above figures are given in greater detail:—

Statement showing the number of holdings in Gaya District.

NAME OF THÁNA.	Total number of holdings examined.	NUMBER OF HOLDINGS—							
		Up to and including 5 bighas.	From 5 and up to and including 10 bighas.	From 10 up to and including 20 bighas.	From 20 up to and including 50 bighas.	From 50 up to and including 100 bighas.	From 100 up to and including 200 bighas.	Exceeding 200 bighas.	
1	2	3	4	5	6	7	8	9	10
1. Tikari	298	148	52	56	39	3	...	...	
2. Gaya	253	163	43	32	14	1	...	...	
3. Rajauli, Sherghati, and Lakhaipur.	331	196	64	63	8	...	...	...	
4. Nawádah, Atari, and Pakribarwan.	546	329	83	65	61	8	...	...	
5. Jahanabad and Arwal	250	119	72	38	20	1	...	...	
6. Aurangabad, Daudnagar, and Nabinagar.	438	144	77	104	97	14	2	...	
Total ...	2,116	1,099	391	358	239	27	2	...	
Add figures from Government estates.	1,533	674	402	280	142	31	3	1	
Total ...	3,649	1,773	793	638	381	58	5	1	
	...	48·5	21·7	17·4	10·4	1·5	·1	·02	

CHAPTER IX.

On The Profits of Cultivation.

ONE of the most remarkable facts about cultivation in Gaya is that it does not, as a rule, pay for its expenses; that is to say, if we take the total value of the produce of a holding, and deduct from it the rent payable and the cost of production, less the value of the cultivator's own labour, the balance which represents the net profit to the cultivator will not give a family of six people sufficient clothing and two full meals a day, if the holding is less than 20 local bighas (12½ acres). In other words, a holding of 12½ acres is the smallest which in the most fertile portion of the district will support an average family of the district. If a cultivator, with an average family, has a smaller holding than that, he and his family must either eat less than two full meals a day, or have supplemental sources of income, and perhaps, even with such supplemental sources of income, he may not have enough food and clothing. It will be shown that the latter is often the case.

In the following figures the average outturn of 3,649 holdings has been calculated out. They are founded partly on the actual figures of our Government estates for 1886-87 and 1887-88, partly on road cess returns, partly on the figures of *sir* villages in the Tikari estate for the Fasli year 1294 (A.D. 1886-87), and lastly on figures given to the writer by private zamindars for the years 1293, 1294 and 1295 Fasli (A.D. 1885-86, 1886-87, and 1887-88).*

It should be remembered that, as shown in Chapter VII, a family of six persons should spend Rs. 93, and a family of four persons Rs. 61-12 per annum, if each member gets two meals a day and has moderate comforts; that is to say, that the average annual expenditure is about Rs. 15 per head, excluding infants in arms.

The following figures, as already explained, deal with averages of large numbers. Individual cases, as examples, will be subsequently dealt with.

In the chapter on the produce of the soil the district has been divided into four tracts—the fertile, the moderately fertile, the less fertile, and the infertile. Specimen accounts will here be given of the first two tracts. If the cultivation of the land, in small holdings, does not pay its expenses in them, it is manifest that it will not pay its expenses in the others. The accounts are given in the abstract in foot-notes, and in detail in appendixes A to G to this chapter.

A.—The fertile tract.

(*a*) In a holding of 5 local bighas (3¼ acres) the net income is Rs. 43-2, which is not sufficient even for a family of four people (costing Rs. 61-12.)†

---

* The Government year commences in April, so that the year 1886-87 runs from 1st April 1886 to 31st March 1887. The Fasli year, however, commences about the 15th September, so that the Fasli year 1294 (1886-87) commences on 15th September 1886 and ends on 14th September 1887 A.D. This must be borne in mind in considering the above dates.

† The abstract calculation is as follows :—

	Rs. A. P.	Rs. A. P.	Rs. A. P.
Total outturn valued at	...	...	62 8 0
Deduct outgoings—Rent	...	21 2 0	
Cost of production	23 4 0		
Less value of cultivator's own labour	25 0 0		
Net cost of production	...	—1 12 0	
Net outgoings	...	...	19 6 0
Balance ...	...	...	43 2 0

In this case it will be observed that, allowing for the value of the cultivator's own labour, the cost of production shows an actual profit. This means that a holding of 5 bighas is not sufficient to occupy a cultivator's whole family, and that he makes some of his income by working as a hired labourer elsewhere. It is impossible, in a series of averages, to separate out the value of this hired labour.

(*b*) In a holding of 10 bighas (6¼ acres) the net income is Rs. 58-8, which nearly covers the expenses of a family of four persons (Rs. 61-12), but will not cover the expenses of six persons (Rs. 93), which is the average size of a family in this district.*

(*c*) In a holding of 20 bighas (12½ acres) the net income is Rs. 78-13, which would probably be increased, in the case of such a substantial *raiyat*, by profits from cattle rearing, so that he would just be able to support a family of six at a cost of Rs. 93.†

B.—The moderately fertile tract.

(*d*) In a holding of 5 bighas (3⅛ acres) the net income is Rs. 37, which is not sufficient even for a family of four persons costing Rs. 61-12 per annum.‡

---

* The abstract calculation is as follows :—

	Rs. A. P.	Rs. A. P.	Rs. A. P.
Total outturn valued at	...	...	121 0 0
Deduct outgoings—Rent	...	43 0 0	
Cost of production	44 8 0		
Less value of cultivator's own labour	25 0 0		
Net cost of production	...	19 8 0	
Total outgoings	...	...	62 8 0
Balance ...	...	...	58 8 0

† The abstract calculation is as follows :—

		Rs. A. P.	Rs. A. P.
Total outturn valued at	...	...	256 4 0
Deduct outgoings—Rent	...	00 3 0	
Cost of production	...	88 4 0	
Total outgoings	...	...	177 7 0
Balance ...	...	...	78 13 0

In this case the value of the outturn includes the sale of surplus straw, as the holding is a large one and could afford it. But, on the other hand, the wages of the cultivator's own labour cannot be allowed for, as a man holding 20 bighas could not do much work himself. He would have to supervise.

‡ The abstract calculation is as follows :—

	Rs. A. P.	Rs. A. P.	Rs. A. P.
Total outturn valued at	...	...	52 0 0
Deduct outgoings—Rent	...	16 12 0	
Cost of production	23 4 0		
Less value of cultivator's own labour	25 0 0		
Net cost of production	...	—1 12 0	
Net outgoings	...	...	15 0 0
Balance ...	...	...	37 0 0

(*e*) In a holding of 10 bighas (6¼ acres) the net income is Rs. 47, which will not cover the expenses of a family of four persons.*

(*f*) In a holding of 20 bighas (12½ acres) the net income is Rs. 62-8, which just covers the expenses of a family of four persons.†

(*g*) In a holding of 50 bighas (31¼ acres) the net income is Rs. 173, which is ample for a large family.‡

These figures bring us to the following results. We know that—

A.—48 per cent. of the cultivators have holdings of 5 bighas (3⅛ acres) and under.

22 per cent. have holdings of from 5 to 10 bighas (6¼ acres).

17 per cent. have holdings of from 10 to 20 bighas (12½ acres).

10 per cent. have holdings of 20 to 50 bighas (31¼ acres).

B.—Nowhere will a holding of 5 bighas (3⅛ acres) support a cultivator and his family.

In favoured localities a holding of 10 bighas (6¼ acres) will support a small family, but not one of the average families of the district.

In less favoured localities, a holding of 20 bighas (12½ acres) will do the same, while in the best part of the country it will support a normal family.

A holding of 50 bighas supports a normal family in comfort.

---

* The abstract calculation is as follows :—

	Rs. A. P.	Rs. A. P.	Rs. A. P.
Total outturn valued at	...	...	100 0 0
Deduct outgoings—Rent	...	33 8 0	
Cost of production	44 8 0		
Less value of cultivator's own labour	25 0 0		
Net cost of production	...	19 8 0	
Net outgoings	...	...	53 0 0
Balance ...	...	...	47 0 0

† The abstract calculation is as follows :—

	Rs. A. P.	Rs. A. P.
Total outturn valued at	...	223 8 0
Deduct outgoings—Rent	72 12 0	
Cost of production	88 4 0	
Total outgoings	...	161 0 0
Balance	...	62 8 0

‡ The abstract calculation is as follows :—

	Rs. A. P.	Rs. A. P.
Total outturn valued at	...	571 4 0
Deduct outgoings—Rent	183 0 0	
Cost of cultivation	214 14 0	397 14 0
Balance	...	173 6 0

In calculating the value of the outturn in this case, an allowance was made for the sale of surplus straw.

Therefore—

C.—48 per cent. of the holdings will not of themselves support their cultivators.

22 per cent. may under favourable circumstances support a small family.

17 per cent. will with difficulty support an average family.

Only the remaining 13 per cent. support their owners in comfort.

In other words, *if we exclude other sources of income,* 70 per cent. of the holdings of the district do not support their cultivators. Those of them who have sufficient clothing and two meals a day must, in addition to cultivation, have other sources of livelihood.

Even if a holding of 5 bighas (3⅛ acres) were held rent-free (and be it noted, that nearly half the holdings of the district are under 5 bighas), it will not do more than support a small family of four people.

The above figures have been collected with much care. They are not estimates or guesses, but averages of the actual figures relating to over 3,500 holdings; and this is true whether we refer to the figures for outturn, the figures for rent, or the figures for cost of production.

It is interesting to test these results by actual figures. In four villages, with a population of 163 families and 1,210 cultivators, the writer was enabled to take a census of the people and to discuss with them their ways and means. A native gentleman in whom they had entire confidence was deputed to find out from each *raiyat* his actual income and expenditure. The accounts so collected formed a mass of curious reading, and abstracted out and totalled, gave the following result for the 1,210 cultivators:—

They cultivated in all 2,286 bighas (1,428¾ acres), and taking two years, the total outturn was valued at Rs. 40,800. Therefore, the value of a single year may be taken at Rs. 20,400.

The actual outgoings of a year* were—

	Rs.
Rent	7,249
Cost of cultivation	3,853
Total ...	11,102

* In all the following figures of these 1,210 cultivators, accounts for the two *Fasli* years 1294 and 1295 have been added together and then halved to give a fairer idea of what one year' expenditure would be.

The cost of cultivation does not include the value of the cultivator's own labour, which is estimated at Rs. 4,669, so that the total cost of cultivation was actually Rs. 8,522, though the outgoings under that head were only Rs. 3,853.

The net income from cultivation was therefore Rs. 9,298.

The income of these cultivators from other sources was Rs. 5,810, so that the total net income of the 1,210 was Rs. 15,108, or an average of Rs. 12·4 per head. But to let a person live in comfort with sufficient clothing and two full meals a day costs Rs. 15 a head per annum, so that there is in these four villages, which are very fairly typical ones, a deficit of Rs. 2·6 per head, which has to be met by insufficient food or clothing.

The deficit is even greater than this, for the estimate of Rs. 15 does not include the cost of social ceremonies, and the 1,210 cultivators spent Rs. 1,482, or over a rupee a head, on social ceremonies, which must be deducted from their household expenditure.*

For present purposes it will suffice to discard consideration of the supplemental items of income. We then find that for 163 families of cultivators, the net income from agriculture was Rs. 9,298, or about Rs. 57·0 per family.

About these figures there can be no doubt. The population and cultivated area of the villages cannot be mistaken. The villages being managed by Government, the amount of rent and the outturn of each plot of land was accurately known. The cost of cultivation is put down at a most moderate sum, and depends on accounts given by the *raiyats*. These accounts may not have been quite accurate, but, if anything, they under-state the expenditure. Hence the total net income from cultivation in these four villages was certainly not nearly sufficient to support the cultivators.

Thus the special instance of these four villages fully bears out the general statement made above, and founded on the average results of over 3,500 holdings, that in 70 per cent. of the agricultural holdings of this district, their cultivation by itself, and unaided by supplemental sources of income, is not sufficient to support their cultivators.

* The actual amounts put down as spent on social ceremonies and miscellaneous expenses in the four villages are :—

	Rs.
Utrend	750
Páli	466
Pathrá	51
Goh̤ti	215
	1,482

The following statement gives in greater detail the figures for the four villages with which we have been dealing :—

Name of Village.	Population of cultivators in village.		Area cultivated.	Gross income from cultivation.			Expenses of cultivation.			Net income from cultivation.	Income from supplemental sources.	Total net income.	Income per head per annum.	Remarks.
	Families.	Heads.		Value of total produce.	Value of cultivator's labour.	Total.	Rent.	Cost of cultivation including value of cultivator's own labour.	Total.					
1	2	3	4	5	6	7	8	9	10	11	12	13	14	15
			Bighas.	Rs.	Rs.	Rs.	Rs.	Rs.	Rs.	Rs.	Rs.	Rs.	Rs.	
Utrend	68	542	1,112	10,962	1,669	12,631	3,524	4,229	7,753	4,878	2,401	7,279	13·4	
Páli	58	397	767	7,362	1,174	8,536	2,696	3,362	6,058	2,478	2,326	4,804	12·1	
Pathrá	6	50	80	514	276	790	277	216	493	297	208	505	10·1	
Gohtí	31	221	327	1,562	1,550	3,112	752	715	1,467	1,645	875	2,520	11·4	
Total ...	163	1,210	2,286	20,400	4,669	25,069	7,249	8,522	15,771	9,298	5,810	15,108	12·4	

Average number of persons in a family ... ... 7·4
Income of each family from cultivation ... ... Rs. 57·0
Income of each family from supplemental sources ... ... „ 35·6
Total income of each family ... ... „ 92·7

APPENDIX A.

Statement showing the account of an average holding of 5 bighas in the first tract.

	Details of holding on average.	Outturn.	MINUS.			Net outturn of profit to raiyat.	REMARKS.
			Cost of production.	Rent.	Total.		
1	2	3	4	5	6	7	8
First or fertile tract of the district.	*Nakdi.* B. C. Ordinary nakdi 1 0 Poppy ... ... 0 5 Sugarcane ... 0 5 *Bhaoli.* Paddy ... ... 1 10 Rabi ... ... 2 0 Total ... 5 0	Rs. A. Nakdi paddy in 1 bigha, 15 maunds. 15 0 Poppy 1½ seers ... 7 8 Poppy seed ... ... 0 8 Gur, 6¼ maunds ... 12 8 Bhaoli paddy in 1½ bighas, 15 maunds. 15 0 Wheat 1 bigha, 5 maunds. 7 0 Other cereals 1 bigha 5 0 62 8	Rs. A. (*a*) Contribution to the purchase of bullocks. 2 8 (*b*) Fees to blacksmith and carpenter, &c. 1 0 (*c*) Wages of labourer— 2½ bighas of paddy } 4 6 2 ,, of rabi .. } ¼ bigha of poppy... 3 8 Do. of sugarcane 5 0 16 6 Seed of— Cereals ... 5 0 Sugarcane ... 1 14 23 4 Deduct value of cultivator's own labour. 25 0 —1 12	Rs. A. Nakdi paddy 6 0 Poppy } 3 Sugarcane } Bhaoli paddy 7 8 Rabi ... 4 0 Total ... 20 8 Cess ... ... 0 10 GRAND TOTAL 21 2	Rs. A. 19 6	Rs. A. 43 2	

APPENDIX B.

Statement showing the account for a holding of 10 bighas in the first tract.

	Nakdi.	B. C.		Rs. A.		Rs. A.		Rs. A.	Rs. A.	Rs. A.
First or fertile tract of the district.	Ordinary nakdi...	2 0	Paddy in 2 bighas with khesári, 30 maunds.	30 0	(a) Contribution to the purchase of bullocks.	5 0	Nakdi paddy	10 0	62 8	58 8
	Poppy ...	0 10	Poppy, 3 seers ...	15 0	(b) Fees to blacksmith, carpenter, &c., including the price of materials for ploughs.	2 0	Poppy, sugar-cane.	6 8		
	Sugarcane ...	0 10	Poppy seed ...	1 0	(c) Wages of labourers for 5 bighas of paddy, 4 bighas of rabi.	8 12	Paddy, rent of 3 bighas.	13 8		
	Bhaolí.		Gur, 12½ maunds...	25 0	½ bigha of poppy cultivation.	7 0	Wheat 2 bighas.	6 8		
	Paddy	3 0	Paddy in 3 bighas, 27 maunds.	27 0	½ bigha of sugarcane cultivation.	10 0	Other cereals	5 0		
	Rabi	4 0	Wheat 2 bighas, 10 maunds.	13 0		32 12	Total	41 8		
			Other cereals 2 bighas, 10 maunds.	10 0	Seed of cereals	8 0	Cess ...	1 8		
	Total ...	10 0		121 0	Do. of sugarcane ...	3 12	GRAND TOTAL	43 0		
						44 8				
					Deduct value of cultivator's own labour.	25 0				
						19 8				

APPENDIX C.

Statement showing the account of an average holding of 20 bighas in the first tract.

	Details of holding on average.	Outturn.	MINUS.			Net outturn of profit to raiyat.	REMARKS.
			Cost of production.	Rent.	Total.		
1	2	3	4	5	6	7	8
First or fertile tract of the district.	*Nakdi.* B. C. Ordinary nakdi 2 0 Poppy ... 1 0 Sugarcane ... 1 0 Rabi ... 3 0 *Bhaoli.* Paddy ... 10 0 Rabi ... 3 0 Total ... 20 0	Rs. A. Paddy 2 bighas, 30 maunds. 30 0 Poppy ... ... 30 0 Poppy seed ... 5 0 Sugarcane ... 52 8 Rabi, 15 maunds... 18 12 Bhaoli paddy 100 maunds. 100 0 Rabi ... ... 15 0 251 4 By sale of surplus straw. 5 0 256 4	Rs. A. (*a*) Contribution to the purchase of bullocks. 8 0 (*b*) Fees to blacksmiths, carpenters, including price of materials of plough. 3 0 (*c*) Wages of labourers for— 12 bighas of paddy } 18 12 6 „ of rabi } 1 bigha of poppy ... 14 0 1 „ of sugarcane 20 0 63 12 Seeds of cereals ... 17 0 Sugarcane ... 7 8 88 4	Rs. A. Nakdi paddy 10 0 Poppy ... 6 0 Sugarcane... 7 0 Rabi 3 bighas. 6 0 10 bighas of paddy. 50 0 3 bighas of rabi. 7 8 Total ... 86 8 Cess ... 2 11 GRAND TOTAL 89 3	Rs. A. 177 7	Rs. A. 78 13	The wages of cultivator's own labour cannot be allowed for in this, as a raiyat holding 20 bighas cannot be expected to do much work himself, most of his time being spent on supervision only.

APPENDIX D.

Statement showing the account of an average holding of 5 bighas in the second tract.

		B. C.		Rs. A.		Rs. A.		Rs. A.	Rs. A.	Rs. A.	
Second portion or moderately fertile tract of the district.	*Nakdi.*										
	Ordinary nakdi	1 0	Paddy in 1 bigha, 12 maunds.	13 0	(a) Contribution to the purchase of bullocks.	2 8	Nakdi paddy	5 0	15 0	37 0	
	Poppy	0 5	Poppy 1½ seers ...	7 8			Poppy ... } Sugarcane }	3 0			
	Sugarcane ...	0 5	Poppy seed ...	0 8	(b) Fees to blacksmiths, carpenters, &c.	1 0		8 0			
	Total ...	1 10	Gur 6¼ maunds ...	12 8	(c) Wages of labourer in 2½ bighas of paddy and 2 bighas of rabi, 28½ pasaries. 6 ,, —— 34½ ,,	4 6	Paddy ...	5 4			
			Total ...	33 8			Rabi ...	3 0			
	Bhaoli.							8 4			
	Paddy	1 10	Paddy in 1½ bighas, 10½ maunds.	10 8							
	Rabi	2 0	Wheat 4 maunds ...	5 0							
	Total ...	3 10	Other cereals, 4 maunds.	4 0	Ditto of poppy cultivation.	3 8	Total ...	16 4			
	GRAND TOTAL...	5 0	Total ...	19 8	Ditto of sugar cultivation.	5 0	Cess ...	0 8			
			GRAND TOTAL ...	52 0	Seeds of cereals	5 0					
					Ditto sugarcane ...	1 14					
					Total ...	23 4	GRAND TOTAL	16 12			
					Deduct value of cultivator's own labour.	25 0					
						—1 12					

APPENDIX E.

Statement showing the account of an average holding of 10 bighas in the second tract.

	Details of holding on average.	Outturn.	Minus.			Net outturn of profit to raiyat.	Remarks.
			Cost of production.	Rent.	Total.		
1	2	3	4	5	6	7	8
Second portion or moderately fertile tract of the district.	*Nakdi.* B. C. Ordinary nakdi 2 0 Poppy ... ... 0 10 Sugarcane ... 0 10 Rabi ... ... 4 0 Total ... 7 0 *Bhaoli.* Paddy ... ... 3 0 GRAND TOTAL 10 0	Rs. A. Paddy in 2 bighas, 20 maunds. 20 0 Poppy 3 seers ... 15 0 Poppy seed ... ... 1 0 Gur 12½ maunds ... 25 0 Wheat 8 maunds ... 10 0 Other cereals 8 maunds. 8 0 Total ... 79 0 Paddy in 3 bighas, 21 maunds ... 21 0 GRAND TOTAL ... 100 0	Rs. A. (*a*) Contribution to the purchase of bullocks. 5 0 (*b*) Fees to blacksmiths, carpenters, including the price of materials for ploughs. 2 0 (*c*) Wages of labourer in 5 bighas of paddy and 4 bighas of rabi, 67 persons. 8 12 Ditto of poppy cultivation. 7 0 Ditto of sugarcane cultivation. 10 0 Seeds of cereals ... ... 8 0 Ditto sugarcane ... 3 12 Total ... 44 8 Deduct value of cultivator's own labour. 25 0 Total ... 19 8	Rs. A. Nakdi paddy 10 0 Poppy } Sugarcane } 6 0 Rabi 2 bighas 6 0 Total ... 22 0 Paddy rent 10 8 Cess ... 1 0 GRAND TOTAL 33 8	Rs. A. 53 0	Rs. A. 47 0	

APPENDIX F.

Statement showing the account of an average holding of 20 bighas in the second tract.

	Nakdi.	B. C.		Rs. A.		Rs. A.		Rs. A.	Rs. A. P.	Rs. A. P.	
Second portion or moderately fertile tract of the district.	Ordinary nakdi	2 0	Paddy in 12 bighas, 100 maunds, including 10 bighas of bhaoli.	100 0	(*a*) Contribution to the purchase of bullocks.	8 0	Nakdi paddy	10 0	161 0 0	62 8 0	The wages of cultivator's own labour cannot be allowed for in this, as a raiyat holding 20 bighas cannot be expected to do much work himself, most of his time being spent on supervision only.
	Poppy	1 0	Poppy 6 seers ...	30 0	(*b*) Fees to blacksmiths, carpenters, including the price of materials for ploughs.	3 0	Poppy 1 bigha.	6 0			
	Sugarcane ...	1 0	Poppy seed ...	5 0	(*c*) Wages of labourer in 12 bighas of paddy and 6 bighas of rabi, 18 maunds 6 paseries.	18 12	Sugarcane 1 bigha.	7 0			
	Rabi	3 0	Gur 25 maunds in 1 bigha.	52 8	Ditto of poppy cultivation, 1 bigha.	14 0	Rabi 3 bighas.	4 8			
	Bhaoli.		Wheat 128 maunds in 3 bighas.	16 0	Ditto of sugarcane cultivation, 1 bigha.	20 0		27 8			
	Paddy	10 0	Linseed in 1½ bighas, 4½ maunds.	10 0	Seed of cereals	17 0	Paddy ...	35 0			
	Rabi	3 0	1½ bighas of rabi and bhaoli, 12 maunds.	10 0	Ditto sugarcane ...	7 8	Wheat in 3 bighas.	8 0			
	Total ...	20 0		223 8	Total ...	88 4		43 0			
							Total ...	70 8			
							Cess ...	2 4			
							GRAND TOTAL	72 12			

APPENDIX G.

Statement showing the account of an average holding of 50 bighas in the second tract.

	Details of holding on average.	Outturn.	Minus.			Net outturn of profit to raiyat.	Remarks.
			Cost of production.	Rent.	Total.		
1	2	3	4	5	6	7	8
Second portion or moderately fertile tract of the district.	*Nakdi.* B. C. Ordinary nakdi 5 0 Poppy ... ... 2 10 Sugarcane ... 2 10 Total ... 10 0 *Bhaoli.* Paddy ... ... 25 0 Rabi ... ... 15 0 Total ... 40 0 GRAND TOTAL 50 0	Rs. A. Nakdi paddy 5 bighas, 50 maunds. 50 0 Poppy in 2½ bighas, 15 seers. 75 0 Poppy seed ... 12 8 Gur in 2½ bighas, 65 maunds 131 4 Bhaoli paddy in 25 bighas, 175 maunds. 175 0 Rabi 15 bighas, 60 maunds. 75 0 Bhadoi 5 bighas, 22½ maunds. 22 8 By the sale of surplus straw and bhoosa. 30 0 571 4	Rs. A. Contribution to the purchase of bullocks. 18 0 Fees to blacksmiths and carpenters, including price of materials for ploughs. 8 0 Wages of labourer 25 bighas paddy, 41¼ maunds. 41 4 Ditto 15 bighas of rabi, 45 paseries. 5 10 Ditto 5 bighas bhadoi. 2 0 Poppy cultivation ... 35 0 Sugarcane cultivation 50 0 159 14 Seed of cereals ... 40 0 Sugarcane 15 0 214 14	Rs. A. Nakdi paddy, 5 bighas. 25 0 Poppy 2½ bighas. 15 0 Sugarcane, 2½ 17 8 Nakdi rent of 5 bighas of rabi. 7 8 Bhaoli rent of 25 bighas of paddy. 87 8 Bhaoli rent of 10 bighas of rabi. 25 0 Total 177 8 Cess ... 5 8 GRAND TOTAL 183 0	Rs. A. P. 397 14 0	Rs. A. P 173 6 0	The wages of cultivator's own labour cannot be allowed for in this, as a raiyat holding 50 bighas cannot be expected to do much work himself, most of his time being spent on supervision only.

CHAPTER X.

Supplemental Sources of Income of Cultivators.

It has been pointed out in dealing with the four villages just referred to, that the figures given for the net income of the villages derived from agriculture, viz., Rs. 9,298 for 163 families of 1,210 persons, can hardly contain much error. They are nearly altogether based on official records.

In calculating the other sources of income, which, added to the net profits of agriculture, make up the total income of these cultivators, we have not the same good foundation to go upon. The amount given, Rs. 5,810, is that taken down from the mouths of the cultivators themselves. It is hence liable to error. At the same time, considering the minute care with which every possible item was recorded,* the writer believes that the amount (which is more than 38 per cent. of the total income of the village cultivators) is not greatly understated.

So important a proportion of a cultivator's income requires further analysis, so that it may be ascertained from what sources he obtains that means of subsistence which is denied by cultivation alone.

To classify out all the entries for the 1,210 cultivators was found to be a work of too much labour. The writer was obliged to content himself with the figures for the two larger villages of Utrend (families 68, population 542) and Pálí (families 58, population 397). These two villages comprise between them 126 families with a population of 939 agriculturists whose supplemental sources of income are valued at Rs. 4,727 per annum.†

* With such care was each item recorded, that even the value of the milk of the goats of the village, and of the skins of the buffaloes which died, has been brought into account.

	Rs.
† Utrend	2,401
Páli	2,326
	4,727

These sources of income may be classed as follows:—

* Item of income.		Amount (average of two years).	Percentage to total supplemental income.
		Rs.	
Skilled labour	...	814	17·2
Wages of agricultural labour.		18	·4
Service	...	859	18·2
Cattle	...	1,027	21·7
Trade	...	147	3·1
Begging	...	430	9·1
Miscellaneous	...	1,432	30·3
Total	...	4,727	100·0

In this the heading "Skilled labour" refers to cultivators who are also artizans. These men, living mainly by cultivation, are classed as cultivators on the principle explained in Chapter VII. They, however, eke out their living by also practising a skilled trade.

The heading "Wages of agricultural labour" is a very small item. It does not include the labour spent by the cultivator on his own fields. The figures show how few cultivators, who have holdings of their own, will work on holdings of other people. That is work done almost entirely by the labouring classes.

The heading "Service" may be divided into two sub-heads, one (about Rs. 600) is the wages obtained for service in the district, either in the village, or elsewhere, as chaukidars, peons, and the like. The remain-

* Divided village by village, thus:—

Name of village.		Population of cultivators.		Net income from cultivation.	Supplemental income of cultivators derived from—								Total net income of cultivators.	Remarks.
		Families.	Heads.		Skilled labour.	Wages of agricultural labour.	Service.	Cattle.	Trade.	Begging.	Miscellaneous.	Total supplemental income.		
1		2	3	4	5	6	7	8	9	10	11	12	13	14
				Rs.	Rs.	Rs.	Rs.	Rs.	Rs.	Rs.	Rs.	Rs.	Rs.	
Utrend	...	68	542	4,878	732	18	428	732	34	40	417	2,401	7,279	
Páli	...	58	397	2,478	82	...	431	295	113	390	1,015	2,326	4,804	
Total	...	126	939	7,356	814	18	859	1,027	147	430	1,432	4,727	12,083	

ing Rs. 259 roughly represents the amount sent home by members of the cultivators' families who are in service in Calcutta, Hooghly, and elsewhere out of the district, where they are employed as darwans, peons and the like, and as weavers in the jute mills. Men of the *Joláhá* caste take specially to the latter occupation. The Howrah mills are full of Gaya Joláhas.

The number of men belonging to the four villages with which we have been dealing, who are absent on service, has been counted. It is found to be just 0·7 per cent. of the population, and each man sends home an average of Rs. 5 per mensem to his family.

If we take the rural population of the district as, in round numbers, 2,000,000, and assume 0·7 per cent. as the number of people absent on service, we find that they come to 14,000 souls. If they send home Rs. 5 per mensem each, their total remittances are Rs. 70,000 per mensem, or Rs. 8,40,000 per annum; that is to say, in round numbers Rs. 2-8 per family in the rural population. That this estimate is fairly correct is proved by the post-office figures. In the year 1887 money-orders amounting to Rs. 7,22,070 were paid in this district by mufassal and sub post-offices, and the post-office authorities inform the writer that these figures represent chiefly remittances by the lower classes from earnings in other districts.

It will be remembered that money-orders are only one out of several methods of remittance available. For instance, a man may send home money by a friend, or may come home on a visit and bring his savings with him.

It will thus be seen how important an item service is as a supplementary item of village income. Except cattle rearing, it is the most important addition to the income of a Gaya cultivator. Moreover, other sources of income are received in kind, and are only represented here in rupees for facility of comparison, while service wages are almost the only cash money which he gets from sources other than cultivation. It is this cash which enables him to pay the money-lender his debts, and enables the latter to lend him money.

The next item, cattle-rearing, has been calculated with great care. The income derived from keeping a buffalo is Rs. 10, from keeping a cow Rs. 4, and from keeping a goat Re. 1-12 per annum.* Cattle are fed principally on straw and chaff saved from the harvest, and thus a cultivator has rarely any of these commodities to sell unless he cultivates at least 20 bighas (12½ acres). Grass is also cut from

---

* A buffalo calves twice in three years, and gives milk for six months after each calving. It thus gives milk for twelve months in three years.

An average buffalo gives five seers of milk a day, producing Re. 1-9 worth of *ghí* and 15 annas worth of whey a month. Thus, the monthly income from the milk is Rs. 2-8. Therefore the average annual value of its milk is Rs. $2\frac{1}{2} \times \frac{12}{3}$ = Rs. 10. Some additional income accrues from the sale of the calf and the dung; but, on the other hand, a very nearly equal amount has to be spent on feeding the animal.

the field boundaries, and cattle are allowed to graze on fallow land, and on fields after the crops have been harvested. Oilcake and the grains *khesárí* and *masúr* are rarely given, and only to cattle of the best class and of high value.

Milk is rarely sold, except by men of the *goálá* caste and by a few of the les substantial Rájputs and other cultivators. Those better off use the *ghí* produced by their cows with their meals. It is said that the use of the only animal substances (milk, *ghi*, &c.) to which many Hindus restrict themselves, is gradually decreasing owing to the extending cultivation of waste lands and the consequent deterioration of cattle.

The remaining live-stock consists of goats, pigs, and fowls. The first are hardly, and the other two are not, marketable. They are made use of at home on occasions of feasts.

Neither Hindus nor Musalmáns sell cow hides. The village *chamár* gets all hides as his perquisite, and gives plough thongs and shoes to the cultivator instead. Hides of dead buffaloes are sometimes sold for Rs. 2-8 to Rs. 3-8 each.

The next item of supplemental income is "Trade." This is a small one, and is explained by the name.

The head "Begging" does not refer to those who live by charity, but to those cultivators who, like *bháṭs* (panegyrists) and *hajáms* (barbers), are allowed by custom to beg at harvest time.

The miscellaneous head of income consists, amongst other things, of the profits of the manufacture of cowdung fuel, home labour, such as spinning and the like, fish and *jangal* produce.

Jangal produce only becomes an important item in the hilly portions of the district, where the aboriginal tribes have little else to live upon. It is also betaken to by members of the labouring classes in time of dearth.

For cultivators the use of *jangal* produce is limited to the south of the district, where the tall reed-grass growing on the banks of the larger rivers is used for thatching.

The landowner takes half the quantity cut, and stacks it. Cultivators who are extremely poor are allowed to cut what is not wanted for local thatching and to sell it in distant villages. There is, however, but a small demand for it, and the price obtained is merely the value

---

A cow gives one calf every two years, which when a year old can be sold for Rs. 3. This gives an income of Re. 1-8 per annum from the calf. An ordinary cow gives 1¼ *seers* kutcha of milk per diem for six months, value Rs. 5-10 at half anna for 1¼ *seers*.

Allowing for days on which the cow may not give milk, we can safely count the milk as worth Rs. 5 for two years, on Rs. 2-8 per annum. Add this to Re. 1-8, the annual value of the calves, and we find Rs. 4 to be the annual income derived from keeping one cow.

A goat gives four kids in 18 months, of which one is sacrificed. The value of the remaining three may be taken at Rs. 2-10 (two males at Re. 1 and one female at 10 annas). The annual profit is therefore Re. 1-12.

of the labour expended, which has already been allowed for under its proper head.

Fish are not marketable articles, and can hardly be obtained, even in the large towns. They collect in the *áhars* or large irrigation reservoirs, and when one of these is nearly dried after the end of the rainy season, the cultivators assemble and take all the fish in one day.

CHAPTER XI.

Indebtedness of Cultivators.

The writer is of opinion that Gaya raiyats as a rule are not heavily in debt. In fact they live too near the margin of subsistence to have much to spare to pay the *maháján's* or banker's interest. The matter is different with the labouring classes, as will be subsequently explained.

It must, however, be understood that nearly every cultivator has a debtor and creditor account with the landlord or *maháján*, but these are as a rule cleared off each year before the harvest leaves the threshing-floor.

In fact, so far as Gaya is concerned, the much-abused *maháján* is much more of a banker than a money-lender, and advances grain during the hot weather and rains to be repaid at harvest time. He is the Eastern substitute for occidental thrift. He saves the raiyat the trouble of saving for himself, and makes him pay highly for it;—that is all.

Debts are, of course, contracted for marriages and the like, but these are rarely large in amount, and the debtors are generally able to pay off the principal besides paying the heavy rate of interest.

In the Aurangabad subdivision, out of 350 families, 193 said that they were in debt to the total amount of Rs. 6,705. This would give an average of about 35 rupees of debt for each indebted family, and an average of about Rs. 19 of debt for each family indebted or not. Again, in the Sadar subdivision, out of 939 cultivators, 85 owed Rs. 6,816; out of 641 labourers, 101 owed Rs. 2,845; and out of 495 artizans, 70 owed Rs. 1,778. Hence, taking cultivators all round, there was a debt of Rs. 7 for each family, while, taking the cultivators actually in debt, they owed an average of Rs. 80 each. The labourers owed about Rs. 4 all round, and the indebted ones about Rs. 28 each; the artizans owed about Rs. 3-8 all round, and the indebted ones owed Rs. 22 each.

These figures must be taken with reserve, for it is impossible to say how much is merely bankers' advances, to be recouped at harvest, and how much is genuine debt. Cultivators, too, have a great tendency to exaggerate their debts when questioned, and we have no means of checking their statements on this point.

From general enquiries made, the writer would be inclined to estimate the genuine debt of the Gaya cultivators at not more than Rs. 10 per head all round; but this is but an opinion, and is only offered for what it is worth.

CHAPTER XII.

Labourers.

It has been found, by counting, that as a rule a labourer's family is smaller than a cultivator's. It may be taken as averaging four persons, though this is somewhat below actual facts. In order to maintain such a family in comfort, with sufficient clothing and two full meals a day, an expenditure of Rs. 61-12 per annum is required.

Labourers may be divided into two classes—*mazdúrs*, who are free to labour or not as they like, and *kamiyás*, who are serfs, *ascripti glebæ*, and bound by custom to work for their masters. A *kamiyá* usually sells himself to a master for a lump sum of money down. Formerly, this was an actual sale of himself and his heirs for ever, but this having been declared to be illegal, he now hires himself, in consideration of a stated advance or loan, to serve for a hundred years, or until the money is repaid, which comes to very much the same thing.

Taking one year with another, a *mazdúr* or a *kamiyá* has very much the same income. The difference lies mainly in the mode of payment and in the greater independence of the *mazdúr*.

The ordinary wages of labour are 3 to 4 seers of grain per diem. A *kamiyá* who has taken advances without interest gets no increased allowance, except at the season of transplanting, when there is a special demand for labour and ordinary wages rise. In most villages ordinary *mazdúrs* get ¼ of a seer for *lukum* (grain for breakfast) in addition to the regular *ban* or wages. A quarter of a seer a day is 90 seers per annum, and a *kamiyá* therefore gets that amount less than a *mazdúr* in a year, and this amount may be taken as equivalent to the interest on the advance for which the *kamiyá* sold himself. The amount of this advance is usually ten rupees, and the value of 90 seers of grain is Rs. 2-4, so that the interest is about 22½ per cent. per annum.

A *kamiyá*, however, gets occasional presents, such as money for drinking toddy and gifts of old clothes, which the ordinary *mazdúr* does not get so often. Moreover, being of low caste, he can take cooked food, which does not count as wages.

A *kamiyá* is expected to do every sort of work, and at all times. In the hot season he is employed on mud wall building, earth-work, and the like, when, generally speaking, a *mazdúr* gets no work at all. A *mazdúr*, when his day's work is over, goes home and attends to his own affairs, but a *kamiyá* is liable to be called upon to go on an errand, or to be present at his employer's house for any little work which may turn up, even after he has done his full day's work in the field.

Mazdúrs absent themselves from their work when they like, and often go on a visit to their friends or relatives without even asking leave of their employers; but a *kamiyá* cannot do so without paying interest on his original advance.

Thatching work, for which *mazdúrs* are often paid in cash at the rate of from an anna to an anna and three-quarters per diem, has to be done by a *kamiyá* at the regulation rate of 3 seers.

A *kamiyá* is, moreover, paid in the inferior grains, such as *khesárí masúr*, gram, while a *mazdúr* is paid in the kind of grain at which he works in the day, getting wheat for reaping wheat, *masúr* for reaping *masúr*, and so on.

At the time of paddy transplanting there is a demand for labour, and wages rise. Women, too, are employed in planting out the seedlings, the men being employed as *kabariyás* (up-rooters of seedlings), *ḍhowás* (carriers of seedlings from the seed beds to the fields), and *chhíṭás* (distributors). The wages at this season are four seers for a man and three seers for a woman, together with an allowance of three-fourths of a seer of *sattú* per head for food.

At harvest time the rates of wages vary in different villages at from one sheaf in every 21 to one sheaf in every 12 cut. The labourer has the right to choose his own sheaf, and he takes care to make it as large as he can. At this time the women also work, and a man and his wife between them will earn about 18 seers a day for a month.

Taking the regular work, lower pay, the first right of gleaning, and the occasional presents of the *kamiyá*, and the irregular work and higher pay of the *mazdúr*, it may be estimated that at the year's end the wages of each is about the same.

The women of a labourer's family work, as already stated, at the seasons of transplanting and reaping. They also work at tapping poppy-heads and collecting the opium. During the rest of the year they are busy in looking after household work, such as husking paddy, flour grinding, cooking, collecting cowdung for fuel, and the like. They sell the cakes of cowdung fuel in the hot weather, a basketful every two or three days, for two Gorakhpuri pice (a third of an anna). The straw of the sheaves earned at reaping time is sold at 16 loads a rupee to *bipárís*, or owners of pack bullocks, if the labourer is not in debt to the cultivator, in which case the latter takes the straw for his own cattle and writes off a corresponding portion of the debt. Five rupees per annum is an ample allowance for these two sources of income.

Supposing, therefore, that a labourer and his wife are fully employed, his income will be made up as follows :—

	Maunds or Rupees.
At harvest time the husband and wife earn 18 seers a day for 30 days	11·25
For two months neither earns anything.	
For eight months the man earns 3 seers a day, say ...	18·0
At transplanting time the husband and wife earn $7+1\frac{1}{2}=8\frac{1}{2}$ seers for 30 days	6·375
The woman can earn 3 seers a day for 15 days at opium tapping	1·125
Cowdung fuel, straw, &c.	5·
Total ...	41·75

or about Rs. 41-12 per annum, which is just Rs. 20 short of the estimated cost of living for a family of four, or Rs. 4-9 a head short of a theoretical Rs. 15. Part of this Rs. 4-9 may be made up by odds and ends supplemental sources of income, such as cutting fuel in the *jangal* and the like, but the greater part must be met by insufficient clothing or food. This calculation is borne out by practical experience. It is universally stated that a labourer has frequently to content himself with one meal a day in order to avoid curtailment of the food of the children, and that, even when two meals are taken, they are rarely of the full amount.

Tested by the experience of agriculturists themselves, the above estimate will be found, if anything, to be excessive. The earnings of the man of a family as estimated above are—

$\frac{11\cdot25}{2}+18$ maunds + $(4+\frac{3}{4})$ 30 seers = about $27\frac{1}{4}$ maunds. The accumulated wisdom of villagers on this subject is contained in two aphorisms :—

(1) That a *kamiyá* gets a quarter of the outturn of his work.

(2) That the usual produce of one plough (*i.e.*, one *kamiyá*) is a hundred maunds.

This would make a *kamiyá's* average earnings to be 25 maunds.

In the more fertile parts of the district, *kamiyás* are given a plot of land called *pachkaṭṭhá* to cultivate for themselves. It never exceeds, and is often less than, five cottahs (about $\frac{1}{6}$ of an acre). The cultivator supplies the seed, plough, and cattle, and takes half the produce in return. At a very liberal estimate, the *kamiyá's* share of the outturn would be two maunds, making up his total income to Rs. 43-12, instead of Rs. 41-12.

Hitherto we have been dealing with the general question. It will now be interesting to test our general results by specific instances.

All the labourers have been taken in the two villages Utrend (families 99, population 401) and Pálí (families 47, population 240) already dealt with under the head of cultivators, and the income of each man of the labouring class analysed out. The classification differs somewhat from the estimate of a labourer's earnings given above, the headings being the same as those given for cultivators, but the final result strikingly confirms the figures independently arrived at.

These two villages contain between them 146 families of labourers consisting of 641 souls, an average of 4·3 souls to the family.

Their sources of income were as follows* :—

	Amount. Rs.	Percentage on total.
Cultivation	677	23·7
Skilled labour	329	11·5
Service	1,012	35·5
Cattle	172	6·0
Begging	25	·8
Miscellaneous	634	22·2
Total ...	2,849	100·
Wages of labour ...	4,275	...
Total ...	7,124	...

* Divided thus, village by village :—

Name of village.	Population of labourers.		Income from wages of labour.	Supplemental income of labourers derived from—								Total income of labourers.	Remarks.
	Families.	Heads.		Net income from cultivation.	Skilled labour.	Service.	Cattle.	Trade.	Begging.	Miscellaneous.	Total supplemental income.		
1	2	3	4	5	6	7	8	9	10	11	12	13	
			Rs.	Rs.	Rs.	Rs.	Rs.	Rs.	Rs.	Rs.	Rs.	Rs.	
Utrend ...	99	401	2,595	419	142	651	121	...	25	503	1,861	4,456	
Pálí	47	240	1,680	258	186	361	51	...	...	131	988	2,668	
Total ...	146	641	4,275	677	329	1,012	172	...	25	634	2,849	7,124	

Here the annual income per head is Rs. 11-1, and per family Rs. 48·8, after allowing for all possible supplementary items. These supplementary items have been placed first in the above list and distinguished from wages of labour. They come to about 40 per cent. of the total income, which is very nearly the same as in the case of cultivators, in which they come to 38 per cent.

Of these supplemental items it must be remarked that the head of service doubtless includes many instances of what are really wages of labour. It is impossible to sharply distinguish between the two. Profits from cultivation refer to the small plots already referred to and to the sale of straw. The head "Miscellaneous" is specially important, because fuel and produce *jangal* are included in it. In the south of the district near the hills this would be a much more important item. There a labouring man easily makes four rupees during the two months of the hot weather when otherwise he would get no employment.

The other heads call for no remarks.

CHAPTER XIII.

Artizans.

Artizans keep no servants. The women of the family perform most of the household work, except sometimes fetching water, which is done for them by contract by women of the lower classes, generally Kahárins, at the rate of half an anna and about four seers of grain per house per month for supplying one *ghará* of water daily. By working for one hour in the morning and two hours in the afternoon, such a woman can earn about nine annas and about half a maund of grain per month. In other respects the women of the family do the household work and prepare the food. Girls are initiated from an early age into the mysteries of the *ménage*, and take an active part in it. The elder sisters, although of tender age, themselves share in nursing, rearing, and amusing the infants of the family, while the matrons are up and about their household occupations.

Taken as a whole, the artizan classes of this district are well off, and are able to get sufficient to support themselves and their families by plying their trades. Exceptional cases of course occur, where the workers of a house are few and the eaters are many; but as a rule artizans and their families have enough to eat. We are now dealing with artizans who are actually practising their respective trades, and not of men of the artizan castes. Many men of these castes have abandoned their caste trades and taken to agriculture or to field labour. The actual number of working artizans is limited by the demand, and hence there is no over-supply tending to diminish their wages.

We now proceed to deal with the principal artizan classes one by one.

The goldsmith.

The goldsmith is paid at from two pice to two annas (generally about five pice) per rupee weight (or *bharí*) of the silver ornaments which he makes, the rate increasing with the purity of the silver. For working in gold he usually charges one rupee for each tola weight of the precious metal. He is also said to make large illicit gains out of the silver and gold entrusted to him, a considerable portion of which he steals. He is not to be seen in every village, as no single village can support him. Generally he is found in about one village out of a dozen. Between sunrise and sunset he is employed for about nine hours in his shop, and in addition for two or three, or (when there is press of work or stolen property to be melted down) more hours at night. A goldsmith of moderate abilities can turn out work which would bring him about Rs. 10 per month in the country or about Rs. 15 in the town. The implements necessary are given in detail in *Bihár Peasant Life*, and a complete set costs about Rs. 5. The handiwork has no pretensions to neatness or elegance, but it is extraordinary what proportionately fine work can be turned out with implements of such rude construction as are in use among them.

The carpenter.

The carpenter earns three to four annas a day from non-cultivators, one anna to one anna and six pie a day, and a *sídhá* (which usually consists of 12 chitaks of rice, 4 chitaks of pulse and a little salt and vegetables), besides about a maund of grain per plough per year for making and repairing it. The tools ordinarily required by a village carpenter are a large cross-cut saw, a hand-saw, an adze, a drill, and a file to sharpen his saws. Occasionally he uses others. It is remarkable what adepts some carpenters are in the use of the adze: so much so that a plane is hardly needed. A full list of the tools used by carpenters will be found in *Bihár Peasant Life*, and a set costs about Rs. 4-8 or Rs. 5.

The blacksmith.

The blacksmith does not usually work on daily labour, as he cannot leave his anvil. His usual charge is one anna per seer on the weight of the articles made. From cultivators keeping their own ploughs he gets the same yearly allowance as the carpenter, viz., a maund for each plough, worth, say, a rupee. He must accept every kind of grain produced by the cultivator, who must, however, give half the amount in paddy.

A blacksmith's shop of any pretensions requires at least two skilled workmen and an assistant who does the drudgery, blows the bellows, assists with the hammer, and does the rough filing and such work. The forge is usually a hole in the ground, with a pipe communicating with the nozzle of the bellows. The anvil is a rude lump of iron weighing from 30 to 80 pounds. Those made by the blacksmiths themselves are never tempered on the surface. If by chance one turns out good, it lasts eight or ten years, but they generally have flaws on the metal, and crack or otherwise become useless in a year or two. A complete list of the implements used by him will be found in *Bihár Peasant Life*, and a set of 13 of the more useful ones costs about Rs. 10.

A smithy of three men, if kept fully employed, would work up in one day Rs. 2-8 to Rs. 3 worth of raw iron, which would be equivalent to about 50 pounds. The outturn of this would be about 35 or 40 pounds, the rest going in waste and burning. The labour price of this at 32 pounds to the rupee would be about Re. 1-4, which, three or four annas for coal being deducted, would give about a rupee as the daily earnings of the three men. Generally a blacksmith's wages is about four annas per diem.

The articles turned out are such as the following:—

1.	Kodál	... Mattocks.
2.	Phar	... Ploughshares.
3.	Kúñri	... Well-buckets.
4.	Karáhí	... Pans.
5.	Hasuá	... Sickles.
6.	Chilohí	... Do.
7.	Khurpí	... Spuds.
8.	Bankuá	... Curved hoes.
9.	Ṭangárí	... Adzes.
10.	Sámí }	... Ferules.
11.	Samuá }	
12.	Káṇṭá	... Nails.

In the towns these are paid for in cash, but the village blacksmith's labours are paid for differently. Sometimes the new iron is given with the order, and sometimes its value. The labour is usually paid for in cash, but as he gets an annual allowance of grain, as above explained, for part of his labour, he must keep the husbandman's implements and tools in repair throughout the year, free of charge.

The brazier.

The braziers are, as a rule, a well-to-do class of men. They do not, except in the large towns, compound brass. The village workers confine themselves almost exclusively to the manufacture of bracelets and anklets of bell-metal, which the lower classes use in lieu of ornaments made of the precious metals. Large quantities of elegant brass vessels are, however, made at Nabinagar in the Aurangabad subdivision.

Broken and worn-out utensils are melted down for the purpose of making these ornaments. Two men work a foundry. About eight seers of metal, which cost about Rs. 2-8, are melted at a time. The outturn would be four pairs of anklets or bracelets, fetching from Rs. 3-8 to Rs. 4. The cost of fuel would be about two annas, so that the net earnings on the manufacture would be 14 annas to Re. 1-6, or 7 to 13 annas per man. Allowing for the time taken to complete the work, this would be about 5 annas each per diem.

Besides the crucibles and moulds, other implements, costing about Rs. 4, are used in the foundry, a list of which will be found in *Bihár Peasant Life.*

The demand for household utensils is supplied by itinerant dealers, whose stock is purchased in Gaya and Patna.

The monthly income of this artisan is about Rs. 10 per mensem, or Rs. 120 a year, with which he can well support a family of six or seven persons in comfort with some savings.

The potter.

The potter generally has a plot of land rent-free, and in return he has to supply the zamindar and his servants and officials while on tour with earthen pots free of charge. The manufacture of tiles gives him occupation during the dry months, and remunerates him better than the manufacture of utensils.

A set of earthen utensils is as follows:—

			Price in dams.
(1) Ghará (water jar)	...	...	5
(2) 1 large pot for cooking rice	...	...	5
(3) 1 ditto ditto	...	...	5
(4) 1 small pot for ditto	...	...	$1\frac{1}{4}$
(5) 1 small waterpot	...	...	$1\frac{1}{4}$
(6) 1 large plate for covering pots		...	Nil
(7) 1 small ditto	...	...	Nil
(8) 1 karáhí for baking bread	...	...	5
Total		...	1 anna $2\frac{1}{2}$ dams.

When paid for in kind, about a seer of grain kutcha is given for the larger pots and half a seer for the smaller ones. A complete set may be bought for three seers of any kind of grain.

These sets are generally supplied at the nine following festivals:—

Dasahará in Ásin.
Chhath in Kátik.
Mágh Sankránti in Kátik.
Basanta Panchami in Mágh.
Holí in Phágun.
Chhaṭh in Chait.
Bisuá in Chait.
Sauní Púјá in Sáwan.
Muharram.

These are the regular festivals, but on occasions of births, deaths, marriages, eclipses and the like, supplies are also renewed. Taking an average of 50 houses as the number of each potter's constituents, he supplies at least 500 sets per annum, the price of which would be 26¼ maunds of grain or about as many rupees. The retail sales out of stated times to the villages and to outsiders would yield about as much again. His income, excluding his jagir, would therefore be from this source about 53 rupees per annum.

He makes two to four thousand tiles a rupee, but his work under this head is fluctuating, and more of the nature of a windfall.

The oilman.

The oilman has no fixed allowance. He receives 4 seers of oilseed if he is required to supply a seer of oil. One seer of the seed represents his labour, and he also keeps the oilcake for himself. Besides this he also gets a *sídhá* from such as can afford it. The landlord gives him no remuneration, giving only three seers of seed, and expecting a seer of oil. His trade is usually not sufficient to support him, and so he also lends out his bullock on hire, and deals in grain which his bullock carries from local stocks to the market.

The barber.

The barber has sometimes a free allowance of land for his service to the landlord. From the rest of the villages he either gets a fixed allowance of grain per annum, or a pice a-head for each shaving, if his client is an *ashráf* (gentleman), and half a pice from *baniás* and the like. The rate for beardless boys is half that for grown up men. His wife serves the women and gets *sidhá* for every visit. In gentle families she paints the feet of the women with *ártá* (a preparation for *símar* and lac).

The weaver.

The weaver or *joláhá* is fast disappearing from the district. Manchester and Bombay competitions have driven his manufactures out of the market. If all the members of the *joláhá* caste had to depend on the produce of their looms, they would have died out long ago. At present most of them are virtually agriculturists, and ply their trades less for gain than to keep up old traditions. This class has also taken largely to service and trade; and the writer remembers that when he was in North Bhágalpur some years ago the *pálkí* bearers were all *Joláhás*. Only the poorest of them weave cloth for wages. What they weave is the cheap, strong, coarse kind, known as *motiyá*. The rates are generally 1½ Gorakhpuri pice (3·6 pie) per yard, 12 *girahs* (27 inches) in width, or 2 pice (4·8 pie) per yard, 2 cubits in width. Sometimes he gets a little more than these rates. The thread is supplied to him by his customers. He is sometimes paid at the rate of about 1½ seers of grain for every seer of texture he has to weave. For every seer of texture 17 chitaks of thread are required, one chitak being allowed for wastage in brushing the warp. A quarter of a seer (pucka) of thread produces a square yard of cloth of ordinary thickness.

A loom costs about Rs. 2-4. A piece of cloth measures about 18 yards, and takes one person about three days to manufacture. At 4·8 pies per yard, this would be less than eight annas for the three days work. Nowadays a family of *Joláhás* has seldom more than one loom at work at a time. Formerly the number was only limited by that of the members of the family who would work.

The shepherd.

The shepherd or *gaṛérí* keeps a flock of sheep numbering 50 to 500 or more.

He plies a brisk business with middlemen, who take sheep to the large marts, especially Calcutta. The rams are castrated when they are about six or seven months old, the demand for wethers being larger than for females and uncut males. The castrated lambs are not sold till they are nearly two years old.

The sheep are usually sold in flocks of twenty, fetching an average of Rs. 30 per score; but when they are picked animals, including a large proportion of wethers, the price rises to Rs. 40 or Rs. 50.

Sheep are shorn three times a year, in Kátik (October-November), Phágun (February-March), and Akháṛh (June-July). The wool is not sold unless it is too much for the family to work into blankets. A flock of 100 sheep yields about 60 pounds of wool in the year, the value of which would be nearly Rs. 11. The outturn would be 15 blankets which would be sold for Re. 1-8 each, or Rs. 22-8 for the 15. A *gaṛérí* with a flock of 100 sheep would sell about sixty in the year. His annual income would therefore be—

		Rs.	A.	P.
Sale-proceeds of 60 sheep	...	90	0	0
Outturn of blankets ...	...	22	8	0
Sale of skins of animal dying	...	2	8	0
Total	...	115	0	0

The animals that die are eaten by the *gaṛérís*.

The flesh of the sheep is not esteemed by the *Biháris*, who consider it too stimulating a food. The goat is preferred. Sheep are taken to Calcutta on foot by the Grand Trunk Road. They proceed by slow marches, but some of them are sure to die on the road. The drivers get something for folding them in fields, when resting by the way, on account of the dung, which is a rich manure.

As stated above, the income of a *gaṛérí* with a flock of 100 is about Rs. 115, which amount is quite sufficient to support a family of six or seven persons in comfort.

The dyer.

Like the weavers, the dyer or *Rangrez* is feeling the effects of European competition. Cheap European dyes can be bought for a pice in the bazar, and people dye their own clothes.

The profession of dyer is in fact disappearing, and with it the beautiful old permanent Indian dyes.

Leather worker.

The village leather-worker (*chamár*) gets 12 seers kutcha of grain annually for every plough in the village. He has in return to supply and to keep in repair the leather straps of the plough yokes. To cultivators he supplies shoes at the rate of one anna a pair, for which the non-cultivators will have to pay two to four annas or upwards, according to quality. He is entitled to the skin of all cattle dying in the village, and in return he often gets a beating when suspected of poisoning cattle. He nevertheless even then considers himself a gainer by the bargain, as he has only to supply three or four pairs of shoes to the owner of the cattle in return for the skin. He is also the village drummer, and his wife is the village midwife. She gets one anna and two *sídhás* a day for her services, besides presents of money and clothes when discharged. The reward is sometimes very handsome, if she assists at the introduction of a male member into an opulent family.

Although shoes are not generally worn by the poorest classes, yet there is scarcely a man who does not possess a pair for purposes of display on special occasions.

The implements of the leather-worker's trade are few, and are so large and coarse that fine work with them is impossible.

Country-made shoes are not made of real leather, but of half-dressed hide. It takes the maker two days to turn out one pair of shoes, and his earnings may be estimated at from two to three annas per diem.

Chamárs have usually territorial limits, according to which each claims the hides of dead cattle.

The basket weaver.

The basket weaver.—*Dóms* monopolize this trade. It includes the manufacture of sieves, winnowing fans, and the like household articles. Like chamárs and sacerdotal Brahmans, they have territorial jurisdictions. They live partly by their trade, partly by thieving, and partly on the table leavings of all classes, except *dhobís*, within their jurisdictions. So deep is their repugnance to the washerman's food, that, in a solemn affirmation, a common saying is "If I do so, may I be like the man who has eaten from a *dhobí*."

The average income of this unfortunante class it is impossible to ascertain. Their's may truly be called a hand-to-mouth existence.

The washerman.

The washerman or *dhobí* has no free allowance of land. He gets sometimes half a pice and sometimes a pice (two to four pies) for every piece of cloth he washes. Well-to-do cultivators usually give him an agreed upon allowance of grain annually, the quantity being determined according to the average number of clothes washed. In the south of the district, the *dhobí* is also the hewer and splitter of wood. How this has come about, the writer is unable to explain.

The result of this survey of the principal classes of artizans of the district shows that, with the exception of weavers and dyers, the handicrafts are flourishing, and those who practise them are, as a rule, able to support themselves by their means.

The weavers and dyers are becoming merged in the flood of labourers, of whom there are already too many in the district.

It will now be interesting to test our general statements by specific instances. All the artizans have been taken in the two villages of Utrend (families 29, population 211) and Pálí (families 67, population 284) already dealt with under the heads of cultivators and labourers, and the income of each man of the artizan class analysed out.

These two villages contain between them 96 families of artizans consisting of 495 souls, or an average of 5·1 souls to the family. Their sources of income were as follows *:—

	Amount.	Percentage (approximate) on total.
	Rs.	
Cultivation	339	11·0
Wages of labour ...	852	27·8
Service	828	27·5
Cattle	60	1·9
Trade	834	27·2
Begging	55	1·7
Miscellaneous	90	2·9
	3,058	100·
Wages of skilled labour ...	3,862	
Total ...	6,920	

* Divided thus, village by village :—

NAME OF VILLAGE.	POPULATION OF ARTIZANS.		Income from skilled trade.	SUPPLEMENTAL INCOME OF ARTIZANS DERIVED FROM—								Total income of artizans.	REMARKS.
	Families.	Heads.		Net profits of cultivation.	Wages of labour.	Service.	Cattle.	Trade.	Begging.	Miscellaneous.	Total supplemental income.		
1	2	3	4	5	6	7	8		10	11	12	13	14
			Rs.	Rs.	Rs.	Rs.	Rs.	Rs.	Rs.	Rs.	Rs.	Rs.	
Utrend ...	29	211	1,217	141	475	607	12	24	55	90	1,404	2,621	
Pálí ...	67	284	2,645	198	377	221	48	810	...	...	1,654	4,299	
Total ...	96	495	3,862	339	852	828	60	834	55	90	3,058	6,920	

The average income is, therefore, about Rs. 14 per head,* or Rs. 70 per family. This is more than we have noted in the case of labourers or cultivators. It will also be seen that supplemental items are a more important item than in the case of either cultivators (38 per cent.) or labourers (40 per cent.). In the case of artizans they represent about 44 per cent of the total income.

These items have all been explained under the head of cultivators. The principal heads, it will be seen, are wages of labour, service, and trade. With regard to the first, it is earned by the field labour of members of the family at odd times, especially at transplanting and harvest; the second requires no further explanation, and the third is only what might be expected.

CHAPTER XIV.

Beggars.

THE communal system of native life does much to reduce mendicancy. We must, however, exclude from consideration the large number of professional religious beggars who wander about India from one district to another, or who congregate in the narrow streets of Gaya town, making money out of the exhibition of loathsome disease. The residue is small. In a population of 10,633 only 26 persons, or 0·2 per cent., were found to be dependent on charity. Taking this percentage for the whole district, we should find the total number of permanent resident beggars to be about 4,200. This number is liable to be increased at harvest time, when people are charitably disposed, and when the lazy, or men (such as barbers) whose caste authorise them to do so, take advantage of this disposition.

CHAPTER XV.

General Remarks.

IT will be seen from the foregoing remarks that in Gaya district all persons of the labouring classes, and 10 per cent. of the cultivating and artizan classes, may be considered as insufficiently clothed or insufficiently fed or both. This would make about 45 per cent. of the population of the district, or, to use round numbers, a million people. It is not

---

		Rs.
* Utrend	...	12·4
Páli	...	15·1

suggested that this large number of human beings is as a rule in actual want of food, or has never more than one meal a day. In the majority of cases two meals a day form the rule, but they have often to curtail the number of their meals for a few days at a time, to enable them to tide over difficulties. When famine prices are nearly reached, of course one meal a day does become the rule. It is the elders that suffer in these cases, the children, except in extreme necessity, reaping the benefit of that parental affection which is the great charm of an Indian home. As one of the witnesses examined for the purposes of this enquiry put it, "The children always get their two meals; we cannot see them die."

The poorest classes cannot indulge in a rice meal, even in the most prosperous localities and seasons, more than once or twice a week. "We know he is a thief," a witness once said to the writer, "because he does little work and eats rice." Their usual food is parched grain or *sattú* at the day meal, and *bhát* (porridge) or *roṭí* (cakes) of the inferior grains, such as *khesárí, maruá*, barley, &c., for the night meal. *Khesárí* is sometimes very unwholesome, being said to produce a paralysis caused by an ergot which is not rendered innocuous except by long cooking.

The labouring classes and artizans get better grains (wheat, rice, &c.) to eat at times than one would imagine, owing to the system of giving a fixed share of each crop harvested in payment of dues. *Kamiyás*, however, rarely get wheat or rice in their daily wages, and consequently do not get good food except at harvest time.

The consumption of wheat is said to be decreasing, and that of rice increasing. This is due partly to increased pressure of population demanding a more fruitful crop, and partly to the large premium on wheat for export making it too valuable an article for home consumption.

Food of an oleaginous kind (such as ghí, milk, oil) is almost wanting amongst the poorer classes. That it is necessary is shown by the universal craving exhibited for it. The richer the man, the more oily food he uses. The day-labourer's use of oil is very small indeed, while the substantial cultivator or thriving artizan uses it and milk with his daily food to a greater extent. Higher up in the scale, the phrase "oily *baniyá*" has become a term of reproach in Anglo-Indian parlance. During the season, greens are eaten largely with a minimum quantity of boiled grain flavoured with salt. When the *sáwá* grass (*panicum mileaceum*) and wild *makrá* grass (*eleusine œgyptica*) are in season, their seeds afford a means of subsistence for several days. The mango stones thrown away by those more fortunate brethren who have eaten the fruit are greedily collected, and the kernels pounded and made into bread. The fact of the fruit having been eaten by another is not held to make the seeds unclean. Then, again, gleaning after the fields are cropped, and digging out grain from rat-holes, give another means of living for some days. These examples of struggles for existence illustrate the poverty of a large proportion of the population of the district.

When the sugarcane is in season, cultivators rarely take a day meal, contenting themselves with the nourishing juice instead, and, so also, in the toddy season, *chamárs* and other low-caste tribes with a less valid excuse drink toddy instead of the same meal.

The houses in which the poorer classes of the population live are mere hovels, closely packed together in a *bastí*. A family huddles together in one, without the most primitive precaution for preserving what is considered in Europe to be ordinary decency.

The average internal dimensions of one of these huts is found to be 9 feet by 6 feet. They are also low, the walls seldom exceeding 4½ feet high. The owner generally builds his own house, a construction such as one of the above, if built by paid labour and of purchased material, costing about five rupees. By actual enumeration in three typical villages, out of 401 houses, 181 (45 per cent.) were tiled, 127 (32 per cent.) were fairly thatched, and 93 (23 per cent.) were described as "wretched in appearance."

People of this class usually wear *joláhá*-made *moṭiyá* cloth, though five yards of American sheeting, costing 8 to 10 annas, is sometimes used instead. The former, however, lasts longer, and the improvement in taste, which tends to popularise American cloth, costs the poorer classes more than they can easily afford; indeed the women still prefer the *moṭiyá* cloth. There can be no doubt that the substantial cultivators have now-a-days a larger stock of clothes for themselves and their females than used to be the case 20 years ago. Clothes of the same attractive appearance cost their fathers too much.

On holidays, a cultivator wears a *mureṭhá* (turban), a *chádar* (sheet), a *dhotí* (waist cloth), a *mirjai* (jacket), and a pair of shoes.

For the winter the poorer classes have a covering made up of several folds of their cast-off clothes, sewn together like a quilt. The filth of these quilts is often indescribable. The writer has once had one of them in his hands, and will never willingly have one again.

Except *Ḍóms*, men of all castes, even the poorest, own at least a metal plate and a metal pot. The cooking utensils and water-pots are of earthenware. Metal utensils are among the first things to be sold off in years of bad harvests, and as these have been rather frequent of late, their use is decreasing.

The women are fond of ornaments, and wear anklets, armlets, and finger-rings of bell-metal. A whole out-fit of these usually costs less than a rupee. European-made glass bangles are also popular. Very few have gold or silver ornaments.

The expenses at social ceremonies vary according to caste. The following figures may be taken as being the least expenditure which public opinion will sanction :—

I.—Marriages.

Name of caste.	Bridegroom's family.			Bride's family.		
	Rs.	A.	P.	Rs.	A.	P.
Bráhman, Bábhan, and Chhattrí ...	26	0	0	24	11	6
Káyasth	45	10	0	40	8	0
Goálá, Baniyá, Telí, and the like ...	9	0	0	10	15	0
Noniá	7	0	0	4	0	0
Dosádhs and other low castes	7	8	0	5	0	0
Pásí	11	0	0	5	0	0
Ḍóm	2	7	0	1	12	0
Musalmán	34	12	0	48	10	0

II.—Funerals.

Name of caste.	Amount.		
	Rs.	A.	P.
Bráhmans, Bábhans, Chhattrís, and Káyasths	14	8	0
Goálá, &c.	7	12	0
Noniá	3	0	0
Dosádh	5	4	0
Pásí	3	12	0
Ḍóm	2	2	0
Musalmáns	7	10	0

These sums are in each case totals of estimates prepared by intelligent members of the castes referred to. Details are omitted to save space. It must be remembered that the sums given are the least which can be spent.

The cattle of Gaya district are, for the most part, insufficiently fed, more so even than in other districts of the province. The extremely arid nature of the climate reduces the supply of edible grass to its narrowest limits. In the hot weather the cattle spend the day licking the dry roots of the grass on the parched-up common lands, and in the evening when they are driven home to the byres they are only given some dry and uncut paddy straw. In some of the Government estates the *raiyats* have been induced to chop their straw for cattle fodder, with excellent results.

No grain is given to plough bullocks, as the *raiyats* cannot afford it, and when the rainy season comes round, the poor half-starved animals are driven out at once to plough the stiff clayey soil. Many succumb under this treatment and die, thus causing a heavy loss to their masters.

The matter is made worse by the short-sighted policy of many landlords who attempt to bring under cultivation every inch of uncultivated land in their villages, which had formerly been used as common grazing ground for the cattle. In the north of the district, the embankments of the reservoirs, and some village roads, are frequently the only places where the animals can stand, graze or take their rest. In this way the health of the cattle and the prosperity of the tenants is materially affected.

Another matter which calls for some remarks is the wholesale use of cowdung for fuel. Year after year the forests and *jangal* whence the district drew its supply of fuel are receding to the south, and as the cost of firewood increases, the sale of cowdung for fuel becomes more profitable. The land thus yearly receives less manure, and consequently deteriorates in its productive powers. The plantation of groves of mango and other kinds of trees, which could partially supply the demand for fuel, and would also supply resting places for the cattle, is not encouraged by landlords. The stiff clay soil requires an unusual amount of constant care and attention to be devoted to young trees, and as soon as the trees grow up and bear fruit, the landlord comes forward and claims the lion's share of the produce. Naturally tenants avoid such an unprofitable undertaking.

H. P.—Reg. No. 691J—400—23-2-93.